RESHAPING REMEDIAL EDUCATION

OTHER BOOKS OF RELATED INTEREST

THE TEACHING OF HISTORY
Dennis Gunning

TEACHING CHILDREN IN THE LABORATORY
Joan Solomon

TOPIC TEACHING IN THE PRIMARY SCHOOL:
Teaching About Society Through Topic Work
Stella Gunning, Dennis Gunning and Jack Wilson

MIXED ABILITY TEACHING
Edited by Margaret Sands and Trevor Kerry

TEACHING ENGLISH
Tricia Evans

STARTING TEACHING
R. Honeyford

TEACHING MATHEMATICS
Michael Cornelius

Reshaping Remedial Education

GEOF SEWELL

CROOM HELM
London & Sydney

Croom Helm Ltd, Provident House, Burrell Row,
Beckenham, Kent BR3 1AT
Croom Helm Australia Pty Ltd, First Floor,
139 King Street, Sydney, NSW 2001, Australia
Reprinted 1984

British Library Cataloguing in Publication Data

Sewell, Geof
Reshaping remedial education.
1. Learning disabilities – Great Britain
2. Remedial teaching
I. Title
371.9'0941 LC4706.G7

ISBN 0-7099-2348-1

Printed and bound in Great Britain by
Biddles Ltd, Guildford and King's Lynn

CONTENTS

Introduction		1
1.	THE CONTEXT OF FAILURE	5
2.	THE EFFECTIVENESS OF REMEDIAL EDUCATION	19
3.	THE SPECIAL CLASS	31
4.	THE CO-ORDINATION OF SPECIAL EDUCATION	52
5.	ISSUES OF SUPPORT AND CONTROL	82
6.	SPECIAL EDUCATION AND THE OUTSIDE AGENCIES	96
7.	PARENTS	105
8.	NEEDS, RIGHTS AND OBLIGATIONS	113
Bibliography		122
Index		132

INTRODUCTION

The economic crises of the late seventies and early eighties have affected remedial education particularly badly. Many teaching posts have been lost and more are threatened. The situation varies between Local Education Authorities and from school to school. Staff on the establishment of secondary schools or working full-time in a peripatetic service are probably safest. Yet where vacancies occur, they are often left unfilled. Much remedial work is done by teachers working half a timetable or less and they are particularly vulnerable. Aware of this, some advisers are trying to protect the better trained. Even where this is the policy, it has not prevented Headteachers from transferring some staff to cover vacancies in other areas. The Headteachers themselves no doubt feel pressure to maintain the examination prospects of the majority, as youth unemployment grows. So in instances where there has never been a designated remedial department, just an informal arrangement to keep bottom stream classes small, group sizes are being levelled up.

Recent reports by Her Majesty's Inspectorate (Times Educational Supplement: 1981) suggest wide regional variations and no doubt the picture is complex. While the policy of providing slow learners with additional help is being abandoned in some schools and staff are feeling demoralized, there are signs of continuing commitment and an expanded role in others. The remedial department would seem the natural starting point for the resource room and the integration of children with moderate learning difficulties. Some remedial teachers and advisers have involved their schools in discussions about the implications of the Warnock Report (H.M.S.O.: 1978) and the concept of special educational needs.

Where this kind of staff development is taking place, the traditional theoretical basis of remedial education has had to be re-evaluated. This characterised the pupil as a deficit system and the teacher as an expert who diagnosed his wants and prescribed for them. In order to match teacher and pupil, the appropriate children would first need to be picked out. In the last two decades screening has been used. An analogy might be drawn with the National Health Service chest X-ray screening which could be relied upon to distinguish the healthy, those who needed only minor treatment and the severe cases. Where more complicated conditions were found, the patient might be referred to specialists who might themselves supervise treatment or merely clarify the problem for the general practitioner. The approach originated by Burt and Schonell has been to conceive of the pupil as having a range of abilities in different areas. Once a case has been selected these are tested in detail. Various aspects of reading performance are assessed in conjunction with other attainments and behaviour. An overall view of the child's needs is formed and a set of objectives established which are then subdivided into appropriate steps. The same tests are later readministered to measure improvements and evaluate the programme. Just how much expertise could be expected of the general teacher has always been debated. The main claims of remedial education rest on applied educational psychology. The remedial specialist has access to a considerable range of tests and prescriptive techniques, but in some cases it will be assumed that they themselves will have to refer to educational psychologists.

Research by Satz and Fletcher (1979), Lindsay (1979) and Wedell and Lindsay (1980) has questioned the scientific basis of screening tests. They calculated rates of false positives and negatives as high as thirty per cent and concluded that formal tests are no more effective than teacher observation. Such research evidence has suggested to Marie Clay (1979) and Tansley and Panckhurst (1981) that qualitative evidence based on the insight of experienced teachers should be used more widely. Not only is the efficacy of large scale formal testing being questioned, so is the theoretical basis of individual diagnosis (Malmquist: 1960, Clark: 1970, H.M.S.O.: 1975). The significance of a slow learner's reading, spelling and arithmetical errors is now far from clear. It would appear that they can avoid them in some contexts whilst competent readers have been shown to make similar kinds of mistakes from time to time. Hypothetical patterns of perceptual or neurological deficits would thus seem to have little support except in an extremely small minority of cases. If the teaching and linguistic context is as significant as the error, the Bullock Committee argued:

> The particular nature of each child's difficulties must be seen in relation to his whole linguistic development. There is no mystique about remedial education, nor are its methods intrinsically different from those employed by successful teachers anywhere. The essence of remedial work is that the teacher is able to give additional time and resources to adapting these methods to the individual child's needs and difficulties.
> (H.M.S.O.: 1975: Paragraph 18: 12)

Introduction

One major aspect of the context of remedial education is that the child has to be labelled before he can receive it. What appears to the teacher a well meaning but objective assessment may have altogether different connotations for the child. He may not see himself or his needs in a positive light. If he feels a failure in his school work, his self-esteem and motivation suffer. For some children the labelling that precedes and frames remedial education may well produce unintended and destructive consequences.

The labelling theorist argues that while the expert may see the child as basically normal, but the victim of certain specific abnormalities, the child may feel these abnormalities have far reaching implications for social interaction. The child reflects on what it means to be perceived as a backward reader. His attitude to his learning capabilities in turn affects his performance. If something proves difficult to learn and is still beyond us after further effort and encouragement, we are unlikely to want to invest much more of ourselves in it. The teacher is also capable of basing his picture of the child on that poor performance and he may not take a positive view either. He lowers his expectations and perhaps his emotional and intellectual investment too. Where the subject concerned are the three Rs, this has profound repercussions for the pupil's view of himself and for both teaching and learning strategies. A late start in reading may make the child appear to himself, his parents and his teachers as stupid, retarded, ignorant or daft. This term 'remedial', which seems to the expert to offer remedy, may put an official seal on the child's and the teacher's low expectations.

Failure in school reduces pupils' life chances. They are less likely to attain a high standard of living or high status work. Given the shrinking labour market, they are less likely to find any work at all. Since more children from working class and some ethnic minority backgrounds have difficulties in the basic subjects, the arrangements that schools make for them may come to be associated with social reproduction. The sociological functions of remedial education have been studied in much less detail than Educationally Sub-Normal (Mild) schools (e.g. Penrose: 1953, Tomlinson: 1981), but it would seem probable that overcoming low expectations, reinforced as they are by home, other areas of the school and the wider society, requires more than many existing remedial facilities are capable of. The efficacy of remedial education has been studied previously and this book takes a close look at the findings. These social psychological and sociological perspectives raise questions about all teaching of low expectation pupils, whether in remedial departments, mixed ability classes or the Warnock Committee's resource rooms.

Since, according to this view, we may gain a more coherent view of what is happening in schools by examining the context of failure rather than the individual's attributes, this is the subject of the first chapter. The effects that a late start in reading have on young children, that pupil failure has on teaching strategies and that perceived inadequacies in schooling have on pupils as they look forward to leaving school are examined. Chapters Two, Three and Four analyse the three main approaches to remedial education: withdrawal groups, special classes and co-ordination of special needs. Chapter Five concerns the co-ordinator's role in relation to difficult or anti social pupils; Chapter Six in relation to special education schools and the outside agencies and Chapter Seven in relation to parents. The final chapter discusses the meaning of special educational needs as the concept relates to those children traditionally the concern of remedial departments. Schools are envisaged as having a series of social obligations to them quite different from those claimed on behalf of physically handicapped children or those with sensory impairments. Hence, although remedial education is to be reshaped, the schools' obligations to low expectation and difficult children are heightened.

My thanks go to all the special teachers I have met or worked with for making plain the possibilities of change. David Lindsay helped me realize how little good education has to do with passing exams. John Wallbridge showed me that any reasonably well disposed adult could teach virtually any child to read. Denis Pittman and Rick Turkington made me aware of the ironies of labelling and special treatment. The children have taught me most. Stephen, Gillian, Clifford and Sarah are my particular touchstones.

Thanks also to those who helped with the book. Rick Turkington, Richard Smith and Jack Gilliland read various parts of the manuscripts and made a number of useful suggestions. Mrs. Jeanne Merrie prepared the camera-ready script. Without the love and encouragement of Lois, Isaac and Jessica there would have been no time to think and no book.

Durham University,

Chapter One

THE CONTEXT OF FAILURE

In constructing a theoretical framework for remedial education, it is usual to conceive of the child and his needs as the focus and the school and its social context as peripheral. Yet even so far as the individual child is concerned, it is quite likely that his handicaps only appear when he enters the educational system. Very few of the children who are later thought of as having learning difficulties have handicapping medical conditions. They seem quite ordinary to themselves and their parents. It is only when they start school that they appear to have problems.

From the beginning, children seem to be capable of reflecting on their learning abilities. What they learn about their successes and failures has implications for their motivation, self-esteem and sense of identity. As soon as they begin to think they are backward at reading they start to learn what that may mean to the wider social audience.

Learning to read is a highly visible social event with far reaching implications. Children also learn who can read as well as they can, who better and who worse. They learn which books their friends are reading and what significance these have in their teachers' minds. The British psychologist Roy Nash (1975) asked six year old children which of their peers were better at reading than themselves and which worse. He then collated these judgements and compared them with the teachers' subjective rankings and their scores on a formal reading test. The children's views correlated more accurately with the teachers' than did the formal test scores. Whilst such a statistical correlation could be accounted for by the unreliability of formal tests at this stage of reading, it emphasizes the degree of pupil awareness of relative reading progress and teacher expectations.

Some teachers make this form of social learning extraordinarily obvious. In a three year ethnographic study of an all black school in the American south, Rist (1970) found that after only eight days of kindergarten, the teacher sorted out three groups according to what she assumed were intellectual variations. The groupings were made on the basis of her informal observations and they corresponded largely to socio-economic distinctions. Each group was given graded assignments with differentiated amounts of teaching time, praise and disciplinary interventions. They were nicknamed 'Tigers', 'Cardinals' and 'Clowns'. By the end of the second grade, this labelling had been accepted and reinforced by another teacher and the groups remained remarkably stable over the three years.

So compelling are the forces of social differentiation that even teachers who profess child-centred techniques inwardly grade children. The American sociologist Aaron Cicourel (1974) found that formulations such as 'maturity' influenced the way teachers promoted kindergarten children. Even where these children were given formal intelligence tests, these symbolic referents influenced the way teachers interpreted specific pupil answers. The British sociologists Rachel Sharp and Antony Green (1975) found the pressures on teachers to keep children busy and make them conform, vitiated child centred practices to a much greater extent than they were aware of:

> What is being suggested is that the child centred educator, with his individualistic, voluntaristic and psychologistic solutions to the problems of freedom, fails to appreciate the ways even in his own practice the effects of a complex stratified society penetrate the school.

Pupils may become labelled whether the teacher accepts the inevitability of this or when she thinks she can avoid it. Another of the mechanisms at work is that peer groups learn appropriate behaviour towards those more or less successful than themselves in school tasks. The American anthropologist Jules Henry (1971) describes how middle class children are taught to put up their hands if they think they know the answer to a teacher's question. If the child does not know, the rest of the class are rarely expected to help him out or wait respectfully while the teacher does so. Competition for the teacher's attention is more likely even when this makes it more difficult for the child who does not know. In one example, he describes how a child called Boris is having difficulty reducing the fraction 12/16 to its lowest terms. The child is urged to 'think' by his teacher and meanwhile all the other children put up their hands, 'frantic to correct him'. The teacher unsuccessfully prompts the child in two or three ways, but Boris is by now mentally paralysed. She then turns to the rest of the class for an answer. Henry concludes that:

> Boris' failure has made it possible for Peggy to succeed. To a Zuni, Hopi or Dakota Indian, Peggy's performance would seem cruel beyond belief. Yet Peggy's action seems natural to us; and so it is ..

Such observations are borne out by other North American cross cultural studies, like that of Dumont and Wax (1969) of Cherokee Indians. The ways in which young British pupils learn about and interact with their less successful pupils have been less thoroughly researched, although Henry's account could be duplicated in many traditional primary classrooms.

The realization of the implications of a late start in reading, or other manifestations of failure, affect the learning strategies of children. It would seem that systematic questioning of one's judgement contaminates perception of detail (Westwood: 1975). In his observation of children failing in Mathematics, John Holt (1964) found that they became less adventurous in problem solving and liable to regress to intuitive or pre-operational thinking. The risk of appearing not to know the right answer prompted them to screen off much of the lesson. Holt postulated that they kept up the pretence of attention by learning to predict when the teacher was about to ask them a question. At this they would jolt awake. If made to answer a question they did not understand, they would fall back on a repertoire of tricks to escape investigation. Nash (1975) found similar phenomena in British schools. There would often be an unvoiced agreement among teachers and low expectation pupils whereby each side would limit their interference with the others' activities.

In a series of studies of the effects of teacher-pupil expectations, Brophy and Good (1974) found that while there are teachers who succeed in overcoming this vicious cycle, they are a small minority. They concluded that most teachers wait less time for low expectation pupils than for high. If a low expectation pupil seems not to know an answer he receives proportionately less time, encouragement and prompting. Even when the ratio of correct answers is taken into account, low expectation pupils receive proportionately less praise and more criticism than high. They are called on to answer less in class discussion and receive less private attention. The mode of teacher approach also varies. High expectation pupils receive their reinforcement in public, lows are seen relatively more in private. Although this form of discrimination is rarely gross, it is constant:

> It appears that relatively few teachers overreact to the extent that they treat lows in grossly inappropriate ways. Also some teachers reach out forcefully and successfully to involve low achievers. However teachers of the latter type are also relatively rare. Most teachers simply respond to (without enhancing) lows' present motivational and ability levels. These teachers communicate minimum expectations to lows, accept their mediocre performance and indirectly (and without awareness) allow lows to remain passive and disinterested learners.
>
> (Brophy and Good: 1974: p.330)

The Context of Failure

Even when low expectation pupils produced a surprisingly good response, Brophy and Good found that most teachers failed to perceive it as such or reinforce it. Nell Keddie saw this as one of the primary mechanisms of labelling in the British use of streaming (Keddie: 1971). She asked the same teacher to deliver the same lesson to 'A' and 'C' stream classes. It was about a boy who had been kept in a chicken coop by his parents and suffered such sensory and linguistic deprivation that he had failed to learn to speak. The discussion with the top class took place at a relatively abstract level and when the children adopted the word 'regression', the teacher assumed they knew what it meant. She did not probe or get them to elaborate their understanding with concrete examples. The 'C' stream discussion was more anecdotal and illustrative. One child volunteered a question which implied a critical attitude towards the concept of regression. He did not use the word itself, but he showed he understood what it implied. 'The woman who put him in the chicken coop made him go backwards.' He then asked the teacher: 'How do you unlearn?' The teacher apparently failed to scan this as an appropriate question. She kept the exchange at a nominal rather than a conceptual level, redefining the concept and offering illustrative material which begged the boy's question: 'Well you simply forget - in schools - the tests show that.' In Keddie's example not only is the child's attempt at original thinking discounted, but the school's ideological commitment to measures of success and failure is re-emphasized.

Whether or not the teachers are aware of the effect of such slights, this constant pattern of rejection communicates itself to the children's affective development and attitudes to school. Those perceived as low attainers are more likely to become bored, withdrawn or disruptive. It would seem safer not to take risks if these merely reinforce a sense of failure. As they grow older, some learn to distrust even those who encourage them. In his study of lower class American delinquents, Werthman (1971) found that most young adolescents were aware of grades as a source of power for the teacher. High grades could imply that the teacher was attempting a bribe and this had to be checked out. Where groups of children realize how deeply their sense of values conflict with the school's, as in Hargreaves' (1968) study of peer group formation in a British secondary modern school, a pupil subculture can grow up in opposition to the official ethos of the school.

This widening gap also affects the staff. In trying to account for it, they build up a series of expectations for their own roles. It may be taken for granted that certain children will present problems and that there is a limit to what can be asked of the ordinary teacher. Such beliefs come to seem quite natural and it may only be a minority who will question them, such as this teacher who had recently left an ordinary school to become a deputy headteacher of a special school:

> The majority of teachers in ordinary schools are worried by two or three children in their class whom they see as problem children. They are anxious to get rid of them. The teachers in ordinary schools are not concerned where the child goes. They just want them out. They don't want to cope and they don't see it as their job. They see their job as coping with the middle of the road child. They feel they can't cope. They are not trained. This child is disruptive and takes up too much of their time. They shouldn't be spending too much of their time in this way. The majority of teachers don't prepare individual programmes according to children's needs. They try to fit the majority of the class into a pattern and if they don't fit they haven't really got the time. (Sewell: 1981)

As this teacher suggests, part of the way such a belief system is substantiated is by reference to training courses or guidance given at the start of a career. In their review of the professional orientation of mathematics teachers, Shuard and Quadling (1980) suggest that experienced colleagues expect probationary staff to be apprehensive about bottom sets. According to their research, many mathematics graduates give teaching too many low ability groups as a major reason for leaving teaching. Part of the rationale was that they had had insufficient training for this.

Subsequent to the recommendations of the Warnock Committee that all postgraduate students should receive a special educational element, the author surveyed the University Departments of Education to see what arrangements were being made. Apart from the four departments where there was a strong tradition of support for special education, the other fifteen or so who responded seemed to lack enthusiasm and expertise. In a few cases, of which the following reply was the most outspoken, it seemed that the expectation of teacher education staff was that students on teaching practice and even probationary teachers should be spared remedial classes:

> Given the very limited time available in a P.G.C.E. course to introduce students to the 'problems' and 'needs' of 'normal' children (i.e. the statistical majority without gross physical or mental handicaps or physiological problems), we do not consider it wise to include special courses in what used to be termed (pre-Warnock) Special Education, nor do we encourage our students to undertake remedial work, which requires the expertise or experience of teaching 'normal' pupils which students and probationers do not have.

Teachers argue that they cannot take responsibility for the least able and most disruptive because they were not trained to do so; the teacher educators argue that they cannot include such programmes because the students are inexperienced. No doubt the well known educationist quoted above was aware of the American evidence that student teachers may be led to lower their expectations of quite ordinary children shown them on film where these children were labelled backward or maladjusted (e.g. Foster, Ysseldyke and Reese: 1975; Salvia, Clark and Ysseldyke: 1973). Yet other researchers have found that the greater the experience, the more likely teachers are to lower expectations to conform to labels (Gilling and Rucker: 1977).

Perhaps the most sinister aspects of the self-fulfilling prophecy are its social class and ethnic dimensions. Early investigations of the relationship between poor school attainments and social class assumed that it was reliable and static (Binet: 1904; Burt: 1937). More recent research (e.g. Douglas: 1965; Halsey, Heath and Ridge: 1980) would indicate that from infant school onwards, teachers' perception of children play a role in the relative deterioration of working class performance. Rosenberg (1965) found that among Negroes from the southern United States, this can lead to absolute losses on formal intelligence scores. Coard (1971) found that West Indians in Britain formed chronic learning blocks. In general, teachers who are sarcastic and humiliating appear to generate higher proportions of learning difficulties (e.g. Nash: 1975) and it should come as no surprise that racial intolerance produces similar effects (e.g. Carrington and Wood: 1981). Where the majority of teachers are concerned, the Rampton Report concludes the problem is rather one of an inability to provide sufficient positive discrimination (H.M.S.O.: 1981).

It may well seem that once a child has been seen as a backward reader, poor, or as coming from an ethnic minority, there is nothing he or anyone else can do to break the vicious circle of low expectations and poor attainments. Yet there are instances of children who seemed to refuse to conform to type. Many labelling theorists have explored the problem of freedom in terms of others' expectations. They have pointed out that there is a degree of choice about acceptance of others' assessments. Erving Goffman (1963) demonstrated how consciousness of social stigma, including physical handicap, vagrancy and illiteracy, may allow the individual to develop a series of strategies for hiding or compensating for the handicap. This may then lead to 'passing' or prima facie acceptance by the community:

> Therefore, when goal orientation is pronounced or imperative and there exists a high probability that definition as illiterate is a bar to the achievement of a goal, the illiterate is likely to try to 'pass' as literate. The popularity in the group studied of windowpane lenses with heavy

> horn frames ('bop glasses') may be viewed as an attempt to emulate the stereotype of the businessman-teacher-young intellectual and especially the high status jazz musician.
>
> (Freeman and Kasenbaum: quoted in Stigma: Goffman, 1963)

Two other American sociologists, Sykes and Matza, refer to what they call techniques of neutralization (Sykes and Matza: 1957). Adolescents hide evidence of abnormality from themselves, partly through psychological denial and partly by pointing to contradictory evidence of normality in other areas of their lives. These presentations of self, to the outside world and to the self may be more difficult for the retarded, but not impossible (Edgerton: 1969). Little research has been carried out in the way such techniques impinge on macro sociological structures. In the case of the semi-literate low attaining adolescent, there must be ploys he can adopt which help him to maintain some sort of detachment from his official school status. He might be free to defeat some of the more painful expectations. Certain forms of teacher-pupil interaction might even allow greater latitude than others.

During the period in which the author worked as the Head of a Remedial Department, there were opportunities to counsel groups of children who experienced emotional and learning difficulties in school. When a special option was set up for a group of children with especially poor examination prospects, it seemed appropriate to let them talk about themselves and how they viewed home, school and school leaving. All the children came from working class homes, all continued to have or had had chronic reading difficulties and a large proportion of each group could easily have matched Cyril Burt's (1937) definition of the 'problem classes'. That is to say many came from single parent families or families that had undergone marital breakdown. Quite a few had had lengthy periods of separation or institutionalization in early childhood. Membership of ethnic and cultural minority groups was disproportionately high. Many had a criminal record. The main objective of this option group was to compensate the children for the rejection and inappropriate teaching many of them suffered as their peers approached examinations.

With one group in particular, a series of tape recordings was made to find out how their attitudes to school, self and work evolved in the three years between making option choices and leaving. Some of the group were followed up and asked what they thought in retrospect. They were at their most positive at the beginning of this period. Most of them would have been able to accept the Warnock Committee's dictum that 'education is a good, to which all human beings are entitled' up to a certain point. Some enjoyed History and Social Studies and they had deliberately chosen these options despite the heavy demands in terms of reading and writing. In these instances it was often the teacher's personality and ability to communicate effectively with a mixed ability class that were crucial. Others had a more instrumental view. They had chosen woodwork because they wanted to be 'a chippy'. Graham, whose view of school had always been negative, summed up another aspect of the group's feelings when he said:

> My dad says school's a load of rubbish. Teachers are rubbish. They don't teach you anything.

Graham had always found it easy to distance himself from the ethos of the school. If teachers thought he was stupid that only made them so, too. His father helped support him in his battles with authority and in his feelings that the knowledge that schools purveyed was fairly unhelpful, anyway. He managed to convince most teachers that it would not be worth their while trying to teach him anyway, which only confirmed his suspicions about their impotence and ignorance. Such a well developed anti-school stance was well appreciated by the group, although only shared by a minority, midway through the third year.

They were quickly disillusioned by the option system, though. After a few weeks in the fourth year, many pupils claimed they did no work at all. This was a fairly flimsy piece of denial and Malcolm contradicted it:

> They're talking as if they don't do any work in lessons, but they do. They know they do.

When pressed about this, the group admitted that most of them did a certain amount of what was expected in most lessons. It was just that where the work itself seemed monotonous and demeaning and where the teacher failed to establish a relaxed, even-tempered working atmosphere, expectations had fallen considerably:

> Pat: What I do is .. I just stick a couple of lines down and when he comes up to see I show him what I've done, he says "At least you've done more than other people have."
>
> Clifford: I only do art if the teacher really pushes me. I didn't do anything until the last moment when the bell's going. He says "If you don't do it, I'll send you to a certain person."

Even where individual pupils had a definite target in view, where the work in hand seemed to teacher and pupils of a reasonable quality and the task intrinsically satisfying, the expectation of poor group behaviour made individuals in it feel that the teacher had failed to keep his side of the bargain:

Clifford: I enjoy woodwork. I've cut out mine. I've just got to glue it together.
Teacher: And you get straight down to that.
Clifford: No. Everyone has a muck about in the woodwork lesson.

Although Furlong (1977) found that with alienated bottom set C.S.E. groups, the copying of notes could make a group feel it was hardworking and purposeful, this non examination group were more sophisticated. The point of the note-making might have been acceptable, but in practice the exercise appeared cynical and unilluminating:

Malcolm: The homework in brickwork and metalwork, there's loads of it, but it's thick. You have to copy it. You're meant to take notes from it, but everybody copies it. I don't know why people can't read it though. That's just as good as copying it.
Clifford: I said to Sam, we've got Physical Science. No we haven't, we've got Mr. Brown. It'll be good fun.
Malcolm: What he means by that is we'll have a muck around.
Clifford: No. Well I weren't there last Friday and I heard they were going to have a discussion like they did the week before I was away. And I was looking forward to that.

In lessons where the group expected to be allowed to 'muck around', behaviour became raucous and childish. In this sense the pupils' ability to distance themselves from the official ethos of the school made them appear even more deviant:

Pat: Brickwork's a laugh. You know, people flinging sand and bits around.
Dave: We're down the other end and those up the top end start chucking wood down and that.

Conversation in the classroom comes to be defined by pupils and staff as something different from and opposed to work, disruptive, private rather than public.

Clifford: What I like is when Sam and Pauline are you know .. then all of a sudden Miss comes over and says what do you think you lot are doing .. and Pauline will just walk away. Then Miss turns her back and Pauline's back again for more.

Wearied by the constant policing, staff resort to making an example of individual children. Tension grows between teachers and pupils, leading to deliberate and mutual alienation:

> Malcolm: When you go into Mr. Gray's lesson, he'll suddenly start shouting because of a few members of this group mucking around.
> Dave: Some lessons you have to stand by your chairs.
> Pat: Gray makes you stand there for about half an hour, doesn't he?
> Dave: He makes you stand behind your chairs until you're quiet. And then someone talks and you're standing there half the lesson.
> Malcolm: Standing by your chair doesn't make you relaxed.

At this period in the fourth year there were still things the group wanted to be taught and aspects of the learning process they continued to find satisfying. But their perception of the inadequacies of the school was of little help to them in locating a countervailing definition of themselves. Whether the teacher was too lax and allowed the pupils to 'muck around' or whether he tried to make them conform, relationships were undermined and lessons trivialised. Very few of the staff seemed to know how to achieve some sort of balance and keep the interest of the pupils engaged.

Since so many of the fifth year staff defined good work as writing and success as progress towards examinations, it grew progressively more difficult to find satisfaction or a reflection of their approaching adult status in their life at school. There were only three lessons in which teachers made serious attempts to advance or even consolidate their learning. Much as they respected the personal qualities of their mathematics teacher, they argued that even he made them do the same sums they had done as seven year olds. On tactical grounds, the headteacher had involved them in chores around the school during the other five options. It was more important, for the examination pupils' sake, to keep the non examination pupils engaged in work outside the classrooms than to leave them unoccupied within them. In this way, they could at least develop an alternative view of themselves as mature young working men.

In the last six weeks of the year, they were asked to write essays on what school meant to them now. Graham, the boy whose father had said that school was 'rubbish', was much happier, as this excerpt indicates:

> I don't mind coming to school because I do some painting and decorating. I am enjoying it very much. I am painting the craft block and the walls. They (i.e. the craft teachers) are very good and we have a laugh.

The Context of Failure

As in many of these 'non-exam' work experience schemes, the work involved was unskilled and repetitive and even though it saved the Local Education Authority maintenance costs and adult wages, there was no financial reward. The only satisfaction that Graham asked was for teachers to be 'good', that is to have a laugh with him and treat him more as an adult. He had finally won his battle to persuade most of them that they should give up teaching him. Although he might have objected to the language, he might well have accepted the concept of himself as a 'hewer of wood and a drawer of water', someone destined to do repetitive and lowly manual work and for whom education is largely a waste of time.

Not all the boys were as satisfied with the way their education was going. Sam wrote:

> We are made to come to school by our parents .. I just come to do work on the Social Area. You would be bored at home. I only have to do Maths and English and Mr. Sewell's lesson and the rest of the time I doss all day.

Sam in fact had a more skilled job than Graham. He had drawn and designed a mural for the fifth year pupils' social area which he and the other pupils had then painted in. Yet the responsibility did not impress him. What for Graham had meant 'having a laugh' meant 'dossing' or time wasting for Sam. Education meant something more interesting and purposeful for him. He could just as well have stayed at home doing nothing, except that this would have been more boring. Sam was in no way the conformist of the group. He, Clifford and Graham were the most difficult and anti-social boys in their year. He had been institutionalized and hospitalized and he too came from a working class background. Only a few days previously a senior member of staff had been involved in a confrontation with him and had called him an 'animal' and the pressures of school life made him as resentful as the others. All three had thought hard about their attitudes to school. Sam, however, had preserved a more optimistic view of the education that schools ought to provide and had made that an important aspect of his criticisms.

After the group had written their essays and discussed the significance of work experience for themselves and the school, quite a few agreed with Sam that they may have been capable of more than painting and decorating jobs. Sam found himself employment before the end of the Easter term and his reaction was: "You never thought I'd get this, did you?" The job was a matter of sorting out strips of plastic and sweeping the factory floor. Yet his position in school, the constant reminders of the insignificance of his attainments, his peripheral role in classes preparing for examinations, had affected his self concept to the extent that even this poorly paid, low status, unskilled work came as a relief to him. Not only was he surprised at his employability, he assumed that the teachers he liked would be, too.

He left that job very quickly for a better paid semi-skilled one. Like quite a few of the ex-pupils from these upper school non-examination options, the experience of work had taught him he could compete with pupils who had C.S.E.s. The earlier discussions had no doubt prepared the ground, but it was only after they had been at work and seen how much luck operated in the allocation of jobs and pay that they could talk about their previous ambivalence. One such ex-pupil, whose father had installed him as manager of part of his launderette chain, explained:

> You know we used to talk and we all said we'd get good jobs. None of us really believed it.

In that sense, even the most successful support groups seem likely to achieve only a partial neutralization of the school's labelling process. The inability of many teachers to achieve an adult working atmosphere, in classes whose pupils feel they have so little to gain from schools, reinforces negative self concepts as failures and poor workers. The culmination of eleven years of schooling may be that many pupils like Sam will be ready to believe themselves rejected by and rejecting of the labour market.

This may well precipitate its own backwash in classrooms. School work may seem all the more pointless if it can not produce a job. Some pupils, like Sam, may retain a sense of the intrinsic value of education if they are given sufficient encouragement. Others, like Graham, are more sceptical. It is doubly important that teachers of older low expectation pupils do not themselves pass on the view that failure at school necessarily debars pupils from employment and status. It may be useful to be reminded of American evidence about the politics of handicap as it affects the labour market. There is evidence that even those released from mental subnormality hospitals can compete provided they are given the right sort of support. In his study of ex-patients in the IQ range 50-85, Edgerton (1969) found that academic attainments and IQ scores were poor predictors of vocational success. He suggested that the immediate milieu in which the young adult found himself, his relations with family, landlord and workmates, were of greater significance. Contrary to the belief that the lower the parental status, the lower the expectation of a job, Mercer (1965, 1971) found poor working class Negroes and Chicanoes more willing to accept their offspring and to give their support to more independent roles. White middle-class parents, on the other hand, accepted official definitions of subnormality much more readily.

> Fully 46% of the parents of the (former) group expressed the expectation that their child would get a job, marry and fulfil the usual adult roles, while 6.9% of the model high status groups responded in this fashion. (Mercer: 1965)

The Context of Failure

Whilst the notion that ex-pupils from remedial classes and special schools should be encouraged to apply for unskilled jobs appeals to most of their teachers, there is resistance to any higher aspirations. Joyce Morris, whose review of Standards and Progress in Reading (1966) is one of the most balanced in the evaluation of reading teaching, exemplifies just this trait. Some of the pupils in her study who had had reading difficulties had found skilled, semi-skilled and white collar jobs. Morris comments that, in this last case, the parents had apparently 'not heeded the recommendations of headteachers and local employment officer'. She herself seems in little doubt what this advice would have been, nor of its suitability. Yet she did not follow up these young adults to see the effect that employment had had on their capabilities.

One of the seminal labelling theorists, Lewis Dexter (1964) compared the position of the stupid in our schools and society to that of heretics in medieval times. Those who earn a good living unwittingly challenge some of our most basic beliefs:

> The stupid who get along well cast doubts on the alleged justification of the system, that it helps people succeed. It is repulsive for some to believe that mental defectives can support themselves, no matter how much evidence is amassed to this effect, because if so, how can we justify the sacrifices and anguish of schooling?

Dexter's article focusses on political relationships as the heart of the problem. Given that many adults previously labelled defectives later attain more demanding and higher paid jobs than those who were not, he argues that compulsory education and universal literacy have an unfairly discriminatory role in modern society. He then calls for changes in road signs, processes of voting and limitations on borrowing and lending rights, and a range of other mechanical and constitutional reforms. In many ways Dexter's theses prefigure those of the de-schoolers and whilst one can only sympathise with someone sensitive enough to the contempt regularly heaped upon the stupid in schools that he wants an end to universal education, one can only argue that the politics of literacy are a great deal more complex and pervasive than he outlined.

It does seem somewhat of an oversight that the Warnock Committee failed to give serious attention to the politics of handicap, especially in relation to changing patterns of employment. It has been criticised by Lewis and Vulliamy (1980) for not including a sociologist. The Committee's overt objective was to eliminate the distinction between the handicapped and non-handicapped and by employing the concept of special educational needs, which could then be applied to as many as 20 per cent of the children in ordinary schools as well as those with severe disabilities. They presumably hoped to lessen the stigma of the most vulnerable. If so, they seem to have underestimated the destructive side effects for this larger number in the ordinary schools. In a society dominated by recession, shrinking labour markets and progressively more technologically complex industries, there is a grim functionality in a labelling process that suggests to a considerably enlarged number of the young unemployed that they could not compete because of their educational handicaps. Special educational provision would seem to have a significant part to play in widening the social construction of stigma, as thirty years of economic expansion and full employment come to an end.

From this perspective, the concept of Special Educational Needs, like the older one of Remedial Education, tells us far too little about how educational resources may be used more fairly on behalf of low expectation pupils. The British sociologist, Paul Willis (1977) argued that where children from working class backgrounds may only look forward to spasmodic unskilled jobs, an education which helps them feel stupid and worthless plays its part in socialising them into such roles. Where Remedial Education is not of exceptional quality, where it fails to call on the talents of that minority of teachers referred to by Brophy and Good (1974) as those who 'reach out forcefully and successfully to involve low achievers', it seems likely that it, too, could help to diminish the educational and life chances of these children. Within school, its role would then be the confirmation of stupidity, the maintenance of a scapegoat group against whom everyone else competes with impunity. Beyond school, it could qualify children from a particularly disadvantaged subgroup of the working class to undertake jobs nobody else would entertain or else drift in and out of work.

Many of the caveats of labelling theory apply equally well to special educational provision as to remedial education and the title of the book refers to this older notion because this is how it is still more generally known in ordinary schools. If it is to have a moral basis on which to survive and grow, it needs to undertake a rather more critical view of its criteria for success, its functions and its resources - particularly the quality of its staffing. Official recategorisation such as that attempted by Warnock is insufficient unless it takes into account teacher pupil interaction and the wider social context of educational failure.

Chapter Two

THE EFFECTIVENESS OF REMEDIAL EDUCATION

The lack of central direction in the development of curriculum and school organization (Lawton: 1979) has had a particularly marked effect on special provision for slow learners and backward readers. Despite the apparent growth in remedial classes during the last two decades (Morris: 1980) there are still large numbers of schools who make no formal allowance. Among the rest there are no less than six broad types of approach. The first could be called the 'basic remedial education' approach. Children with reading and/or mathematics problems are screened, diagnosed and taught in small groups for between three and five lessons a week by specialist remedial staff. They are withdrawn from ordinary lessons during this time. This model can easily be staffed by part-time or peripatetic staff and is most used in primary schools.

The second could be called the 'extended remedial education' approach. The main functions and roles are the same as the first but in addition, remedial staff also try to act in an advisory capacity, setting work for their children to do in other lessons and passing on information about their work to other staff. This might include examples of reading, spelling and arithmetic tests, diagnostic techniques, analyses of patterns of errors, for instance, or a full programme of syllabus, behavioural objectives and so on. The third approach could be typed as a 'special class' although it may well be known as the remedial class, opportunity or progress class, the unit, and so on. Pupils are withdrawn as a group for a wider range of subjects for a proportion of the timetable that ranges from a quarter of the whole. The group might run from the first to fifth, first to third or second and third years. A variant on this is the non exam group. This takes a small group through their last two years at school and this fourth approach is most widely used in 13-16 Upper schools. The fifth approach could be called the 'learning consultant'. Teachers give children from the full ability range short intensive courses in the case of absence or specific learning difficulties in spelling, mathematics and so on. The last approach is the 'Special Education Co-ordinator' who as well as managing many of the previously mentioned functions fulfils a more critical and wider role in developing staff expertise with deviant pupils across the curriculum.

This division into types of approach corresponds fairly well to the matrix devised by H.M.I.s on the Sheffield Curriculum Project (Wilcox and Eustace: 1980) and indicates the diversity of aims and interests of remedial specialists. Correlated in this way it allows us to devise criteria of success appropriate to each approach and to measure them all against the broader issues raised by the sociology of school failure.

The effectiveness of the basic remedial model has been open to doubt since the early fifties (Curr and Gourlay: 1953; Collins: 1961). While there is considerable evidence of short term gains, especially in the skills of phonic decoding and word recognition, there is scepticism about the development of comprehension. Nearly all the subsequent research would indicate (Carroll: 1972) that once remedial provision is withdrawn there is a fall-off in the rate of progress. This enables control groups who have no special help to catch them up. The most scrupulous analysis is by Collins. As the issues he raised have still not been satisfactorily dealt with by the supporters of additional provision, it is worthwhile examining his research and conclusions in some detail.

Collins took as his starting point the concept of reading retardation, as adopted by Burt and Schonell. They had drawn the distinction between a group of children who obtained average or better IQ scores and who nevertheless were retarded in the area of reading and those who scored badly and whose poor reading could be explicated in terms of general backwardness. It would be expected that close attention to the pattern of errors, specially devised drills and therapautic programmes would remedy such retardation. The underlying problems were thought to be in perceptual, psychomotor and affective areas of development. Relief of these would supposedly allow the retarded reader to catch up with his intellectual peers and develop thereafter at much the same rate. Partly as a result of Schonell's work, the Remedial Education Centre had recently been set up in the Birmingham Institute of Education. A number of local children had been sent to the Centre to be treated by experienced teachers who were studying for the Diploma in Psychology. Collins analysed the results of the children before and after their six months of remedial treatment, then after a further year and two years. He found that a group of 116 children of average IQ made gains of fifteen months in six months, but when the children were compared with a similar group who had been attending a local authority remedial centre, there was no overall difference twelve months later.

The second part of the research was a controlled experiment whereby a group of sixty second and third year junior school children were selected from a cross section of ten city schools. As before, the children had average IQ skills, none had sensory or physical handicaps and none was maladjusted.

Many had social or emotional difficulties however, and all had reading scores two years and six months retarded. The children were randomly distributed amongst three groups. Twenty went to the Remedial Education Centre for six months where they were taught individually or in small groups by Diploma students, using diagnostic/prescriptive methods as well as a range of play activities and visits to maintain motivation. Twenty were taught in small groups in their own schools by members of the Peripatetic Remedial Service. They too had reading practice diagnostic/prescriptive materials, but there was less scope for play or visits. The third group of twenty were left in their own classrooms and were given no additional provision.

The short term gains as measured by a range of word recognition and silent reading tests were impressive for both of the experimental groups, yet the rate of progress slowed so markedly after remedial provision was withdrawn that two years after the experiment had begun, the control group caught them up. In the third year all three groups made the same amount of progress. On the basis of this research, Collins argued that remedial approaches based on concepts like visual and auditory perception and reading retardation are 'highly unscientific':

> The accounts at best represent only a beginning stage in research. At worst they are pseudo-scientific propaganda.

His own explanation of the results centres of the concept of maturation. There is a great deal of psychological evidence that premature teaching of some skills, such as babies walking upstairs, may excite short term progress (Gesell and Thompson: 1929) but that other children soon catch them up. Collins argued that reading skills can be made to develop but very probably at the cost of increased tension. If, as seemed likely, the children's long term performance remains unaffected, remedial education is as he put it in a later article (Collins: 1972) 'a hoax'.

There are a number of objections that could be raised before we could generalize Collins's criticisms to all remedial education. Children chosen for remedial reading often attend more regularly and stay longer than in his study, and their IQs are lower. They are likely to include some children with sensory and physical handicaps and some who could be seen as maladjusted. Despite what Collins found to be generally high standards of the Birmingham junior schools in the 1948-1953 period, post war British classrooms seem in retrospect to have had especially low standards in reading (H.M.S.O.: 1966; Start and Wells: 1972; H.M.S.O.: 1975). Children returning from special help might not have had appropriate support. Also, Collins's concept of maturation was based on a physiological paradigm which has not subsequently proved a very promising predictor of educational development. Nevertheless, with very few exceptions, studies of the long term effectiveness of this kind of intervention have shown a similar pattern of short term gains followed by a relative slowing down in the rate of progress.

More recent studies (Cashdan, Pumfrey and Lunzer: 1971, H.M.S.O.: 1978 B) have shown that while many children make short term gains, some do not and a few actually regress. It would also appear that the diagnostic instruments in use can not predict who will benefit and by what degree:

> We still do not know why some children improve under remedial instruction, while others remain non-readers. We also do not know why so many untreated children apparently recover spontaneously.
> (Cashdan, Pumfrey and Lunzer: 1971)

Cashdan's analysis would thus seem to discredit Collins's maturational thesis, at least in so far as it is measurable by present psychological tests, yet it reflects even less credit on the scientific basis of remedial education. A simpler explanation, and one with which the Bullock Committee would have agreed, might be that children with reading difficulties often make progress if they are given extra attention by experienced and well intentioned teachers. Such attention has however a double edged quality and, despite the techniques and intentions of the teacher, may itself inhibit progress. It would also appear that for progress to be maintained after this additional provision has been withdrawn, there needs to be a well co-ordinated school policy for the ability band just above the least able. Morris (1966) found that where good leadership is coupled with the belief that while low socio-economic origins influence attainment, the contribution of a school ought to be that much greater and some headteachers have been able to bring this about.

One of the outstanding qualities of the headteachers of both 'improver' schools in Morris's sample was their determination to compensate the majority of their pupils for the fact that they came from underprivileged homes. In general, headteachers of schools with the most satisfactory results in the survey also believed that although children's home circumstances undoubtedly influence their reading progress, the contribution of their schooling should be much greater.

Although the case studies of the ten most exceptional schools in her survey are vivid, they offer little substantive evidence of the inter-relationship between the leadership of the headteacher, the attitudes of the staff and the attainments of the least able. Recently however a local L.E.A. trial of the American DISTAR programmed learning kit has allowed the author to engage in a year's ethnographic study of a participating school which happened to exemplify Morris's points. The catchment area was a mining village whose degree of overcrowding and amenities, although by no means the poorest in the region, were well below national standards (Dewdney and

Rhind: 1975). Employment was skewed towards mining, the construction industry and transport. There were considerably fewer adults with 'O' and 'A' levels, ONC and HNC or degrees than general for the region and fewer in professional or white collar jobs. Unemployment in the area had always been above the national average and has gone up steeply since the survey was completed. Although in historical terms mining villages seem to have had extended family patterns which have led to rather greater stability and rather less child care committals than is general among families from similar socio-economic backgrounds in other nearby urban industrialized areas, recent housing policy shifts have led to an increase in local movement and in the number of outside 'problem families' entering the village.

Despite the range of difficulties, reading standards are extremely high. The average reading age of the 1980-81 top juniors was three quarters of a year above their chronological age, using a test (Schonell W.R.T.: 1950) whose latest calibration only goes as high as 13.9. With other tests which have a higher ceiling, this average might well have been higher. The most significant feature of these results so far as remedial education is concerned is that no child has a reading age of less than ten. Since backwardness in reading has been defined as a retardation of about twenty eight months at this stage (Rutter, Tizard and Whitmore: 1971) and no child in this survey was retarded by more than eighteen months, there would appear to be no-one leaving that school with special educational needs, at least in terms of academic attainments.

Remedial reading starts in the last year of the infants school. The teacher sees small groups of children for up to an hour a day for three or four sessions a week. She uses a range of basal and supplementary readers as well as home produced and commercially available phonic materials that are wider in scope but no different in style from those commonly used throughout the country. A distinctive difference though was the level of drive among the children. Two or three did appear lifeless and unmotivated and one of them had truancy problems. Yet the teacher was authoritative and dynamic and even when the poor readers were seen in a reading context without her presence, their approach was sharp and full of attack. She was experienced and well organized and before she had returned to teaching after her family had grown up, she had worked as a general teacher. She had undertaken a number of practical L.E.A. day and evening classes, but no formal training in remedial education.

The emphasis of the headteacher was to provide a well organized and highly competitive teaching environment which was grounded in reading and writing. He himself heard the most able readers regularly in his study and had organized an extensive supplementary scheme for all those with reading ages of twelve and a half or more in which the children have to show evidence of reading two books a week at least. The headteacher made clear to his staff that they were expected to concentrate on the middle band and the less able. They were expected to hear them read several times a week and give them help with phonics and other aspects of accuracy and comprehension.

Spelling is arranged on a competitive basis. There is a ladder for each class but each class has to compete with the others. There is a spelling test every Friday and the group scores are averaged so that the least able can affect the overall class mark. Despite the fact that the children's rank order is reinforced, the pressure of the class to co-operate seems to overcome the effects of labelling. Project work is managed from the school's large library collections from which children are encouraged to take home books. Even the mathematics scheme was chosen because it had a large reading element. The headteacher felt that problem solving in words was a more important aspect of mathematical thinking than the ability to perform computational skills.

The headteacher grew up in this village and apart from the recent arrivals from the outlying area, he knows the population extremely well. It is part of his teaching philosophy that he had to fight his way out of a low status role and that education should make that possibility available to all. His own political outlook could be described as democratic socialist and although he has a strong personality and dominates the school, he makes sure his policies are thoroughly discussed and supported by the staff. The pace of the school is hard and like the more successful schools described in Morris's survey, those teachers who cannot take it leave. Despite a great fund of empathy there were definite limits to what this headteacher would tolerate. A few years previously his school had been rebuilt and since then children had climbed on the roof, ripped the slates off and thrown them into an industrial site opposite. The possibility that such vandals could have come from his school and show such ingratitude rankled. The children had been given extraordinary opportunities and if they turned their backs of them there must have been something deeply wrong with them as individuals.

Perhaps the most convincing illustration of Morris's thesis was the result of the DISTAR trial itself. We set up a control group who had originally been chosen to take part but who through some technical oversight were dropped from the experimental group at the last moment. Reading ages and the kinds of reading difficulties were very similar to the others and they continued to have the same kind of treatment as children in the remedial groups had had before.

D.I.S.T.A.R. is a teacher directed behaviourist scheme which provides a script for the teacher to follow. Instructions and gestures are tightly prescribed and the objective is to build up a series of formats - collections of mainly phonic data in groups of pupils. Evidence from inner city American schools (Becker: 1977) and other local industrialized areas (Lloyd: 1978 unpublished) would suggest large gains, especially in the first year of exposure. Despite minor snags like differences in pronunciation and orthography, most of the schools in this survey did better using DISTAR, yet in the case of this particular school, the remedial education group did even better. (Sczypka: 1981 unpublished). This seemed to have happened because of the class teacher's concern to second the remedial teacher's efforts. There were pressures on the class teachers to hear these children read and help them out. This in turn followed from the headteacher's determination to ensure that everyone progressed in reading and from the political philosophy shared by headteacher and staff that they should compensate for the lack of economic and cultural capital in the home. It is possible, as Morris indicates, for headteachers to produce very high standards from a sense of professional duty. It is equally possible for headteachers to have strong political convictions yet lack the power and the organising ability to put them into effect. Yet where authority and attitudes inter-relate as they did in the school, remedial education may be more effective than the most promising programmed learning kits.

It would appear that the power of the primary school headteacher to affect the reading standards of the weakest children is much greater than that of a secondary headteacher (Morris: 1966). In a questionnaire survey of 250 teachers in an East Midlands new town (Sewell: 1981) the author found that attitudes towards stigma and poor educational attainments were a closer reflection of the headteachers' views and more homogeneous in primary schools than secondary. As a corollary of its demystification of Remedial Education, the Bullock Committee (H.M.S.O.: 1975) lent its weight to a language policy across the curriculum. It would be absurd for children to be released from the remedial groups of a secondary school with reading ages of nine and a half - nominally the level at which we can cope with many of the demands of adult life - if the school's science textbooks had readability scores of thirteen. If children have only just mastered the skills of reading continuous pieces of prose accurately and fluently and need to practice skimming and scanning in order to pick out an argument and comment on it, it is of little use if they are only ever presented with short passages, broken up with illustrations, which they read in bursts of one and a half minutes at a time (Lunzer and Gardner: 1979). The School's Council Project, Reading for Learning (Lunzer and Gardner: to be published) has attempted to ensure that comprehension skills are extended in subjects other than English. It would seem essential that if, as Collins and others have shown, rates of progress fall off after remedial provision is withdrawn, part of the role of extended remedial education should be to develop links with a range of subject departments. This is not merely to tell them about what backward readers do in remedial lessons but to extend the scope of reading development through other subjects.

Unfortunately the lexical demands of the School's Council Project material have so far provided the least able with little practical help. Many of the analytical exercises have been designed with upper school examination sets in mind. This is not in itself a criticism of the Project team. They have seemingly attempted to provide a bridge between comprehension and study skills for the more able. Yet early indications are that children who might normally have had remedial education, but who are now in mixed ability lessons working on DARTS material are making only six months reading progress per calendar year.

Another approach to a language policy for the least able across the curriculum is to involve especially sympathetic and competent subject staff in small group reading tuition.

Historically, a large proportion of those teaching the least able in secondary schools have been incompetent or inexperienced (H.M.S.O.: 1971). Despite the growth in status of remedial departments, evidence presented to the Bullock Committee suggested that "work with slow learners seems unhappily to rank low in the list of priorities" (H.M.S.O.: 1975). Given the relationship of education to our political and economic structures, such prestige seems far from an unhappy accident. Nevertheless, this observation might prove a more fruitful starting point for reshaping remedial education. Even if most subject staff are capable of subverting a language policy for the least able when the issue is approached head on and at a theoretical level, it ought still to be possible to make a start with that minority of teachers who, in the words of Brophy and Good (1974) "reach out forcefully and successfully to involve low achievers". Subject departments can be drawn in piecemeal, by arranging that teachers whose sympathetic interest and competence are reflected by these children, to become involved in practical reading teaching for part of their time, whatever their major subject speciality.

In the author's school a meeting was called to discuss remedial reading tuition. All teachers were free to come but those who seemed most liked and respected by the slow learners were invited. Criteria were deliberately vague. These children knew who taught them best and we were guided by their intuitions. In retrospect, it did seem possible to generalize. It was not a case of having teachers who were just 'a good laugh'. Maturity, the ability to appear reliable and enforce high standards were as important as being able to laugh at one's role as a teacher. Some were formal, but not to the extent that warmth and interest in the pupils' well being was extinguished. Most such staff were slightly anarchic, uneasy about identifying with the aims of the system, yet not so alienated as to forget these children's needs to learn as well and as quickly as possible.

Some of those who volunteered found that the pace of work of a small group did not suit their teaching style. Others whom the slow learners thought were good teachers did not want to teach remedial reading. There was the unspoken fear that once a teacher got a reputation as being good with the slow learners he would never be given any other classes. In the folklore of the staffroom the remedial teacher is often seen as rather stupid himself. Where promotion reflects the ability to get children through examinations and where headteachers and other high ranking staff know little about the demands of such work, becoming involved may prove a tactical mistake. Nevertheless, out of a staff of fifty we could get eight or more to take a small group for three periods a week for reading. Timetable commitments varied and some worked for a year, dropped out for two and then came back in. Altogether there was a pool of twenty teachers with experience at the end of the scheme. They underwent a course of practical training which is described in more detail in Chapter Four. Mainly, though, these teachers were competent with all children and while they were told they could ask for advice and support at any time, they were mature enough to find their own strategies as they went along.

The results paralleled the research findings - except in terms of long term effectiveness. Their statistical reliability fails many of Curr and Gourlay's (1953) and Collins's (1961) criteria. Two of the tests involved, Burt and Schonell, were recalibrated during this period. One, the Holborn Sentence Reading Test (Watts: 1949) was withdrawn and one was only introduced relatively late - the GAP (McLeod: 1970). Some had high 'thresholds'. GAP only started at 7.9 so that it was impossible to measure the progress of those with minimal reading skills. GAP and the recalibrated word recognition tests also had low 'ceilings' so that if a poor reader made excellent progress and reached the top of the scale one year it was impossible to measure subsequent progress. In a broad based longitudinal survey like this, it is also difficult knowing at which point to define success. Early in the programme we fixed a reading age of nine and a half as this corresponded with the level at which the local Schools Psychological Service suggested children could learn to cope in school and afterwards, and which predicted a mastery of phonics such that regression was unlikely. Later we found that some children were better than others at coping with a broad range of subjects with reading ages this low and some especially shy or alienated children were retained when they had reading ages as high as eleven. Follow-up work indicated that once children had attained 9.5, less than two and a half per cent regressed.

The main purpose of these test scores was to monitor the children's work, not the staff's. In order to compete with other departments we made ourselves as accountable as possible. Hence a full record of trends was kept. Over the years the percentage of children entering the school with reading ages of less than nine and a half stayed constant, but the percentage of those leaving school at this level fell from eight per cent to less than one per cent and those entering the upper school at this level fell from over ten per cent to less than two per cent.

Re-analysing the GAP scores of the last three years of the project, it was possible to compare short and long term progress from a number of different perspectives. Children were selected from those who had scored 10.3 or less, as the basis of primary school reports and their rating on Schonell by their primary school teacher. They then stayed in remedial groups until we felt they could cope. It was therefore possible to pick out four groups and compare their scores. The first were children who had progressed sufficiently well that they left the remedial group after one year. The second were children who left after two years. The third stayed until at least the end of the third year and the fourth was a borderline group, with reading ages between 9.5 and 10.5, who might have been included if their primary school had been more worried about them. We could measure average progress while they had this additional provision, after this provision was withdrawn and where it was not given.

The average progress in months per year for all those receiving remedial help was 14.4 or marginally more than their chronological progress. For the twenty children in the first group who received remedial tuition in the first year only and who could therefore be expected to have shown the most marked improvement, progress amounted to 22.4 months per calendar year, or marginally above that noted in the large scale survey of Cashdan et al (1971) of specialist remedial teachers. For the sixteen who received help for three years, the average gain in months per annum was 11.7. This lesser rate of progress is also unsurprising given that so many of the group started with Schonell scores of under seven years.

As with Collins, we found that the average rate of progress fell off badly when the children left the remedial groups - 5.0 months per annum for the first group. Unlike Collins, however, scores did not remain static for some time, then move ahead more rapidly. This rate of progress was constant, as measured on a yearly basis. Also unlike Collins, we found that when these results were compared to the borderline group who had had no help, the remedial group more than maintained their lead. The average gains of the one year group during this three year period were 11.7 per calendar year compared to the borderline group's 5.9. In other words, the group who had had one year's tuition had not only overtaken children whose reading was on average marginally better, they had maintained much of that lead. The three year group, which contained children of whom the school had had the lowest expectations, progressed almost twice as fast as this group.

These results suggest even greater degrees of doubt about Collins's theory of maturation. The three year group ought, according to such a thesis, to have fallen away after an initial spurt. In fact progress was marginally greater in the second and third years than it was in the first. As with Cashdan, we found that even using apparently sophisticated diagnostic techniques, it was largely impossible to predict who would benefit and by what degree. We had at our disposal an array of verbal and non-verbal intelligence tests, as well as the Aston Index. As with Tansley and Panckhurst (1981) we found such instruments only gave a 'spurious precision'. This is perhaps most vividly indicated by the progress of the five children who had reading tuition for two years only. During this period their average gain was less than the one year group and the three year group - 8.8.

It is arguable that these figures show that there are groups of children who fail to benefit even when they are taught by staff who are generally conceived to be especially competent and child orientated. Some of the children in the two year group had found it hard to settle in the Comprehensive school. Four of them had been so difficult they had been considered for the Local Tutorial Unit. No doubt one could characterize such a group as 'delinquescent' (Hargreaves: 1967). Yet this evades the rather more fundamental problem that even when a school had arranged its staff resources so that remedial education was carried out by non-confronting but strong staff, it still managed to generate a degree of deviance. We do not yet have the social psychological tools precise enough to predict the effects of institutional dynamics on particular children. It only became clear that these two year children could achieve only marginal benefits from Remedial Education sets in retrospect. Only one of the children actually progressed to the Tutorial Unit and the Psychologist would not have allowed him to be labelled as 'maladjusted'. Two were close friends of another child who in fact progressed to a Day Maladjusted School, yet there were other close friends who did not suffer in the same way, which suggests that this in itself is an insufficient explanation. For a few children, even the use of the most humane and sensitive staff for remedial education is only partially effective.

Another of Collins's major criticisms is that the results of remedial education often compare well with 'control groups' because the latter are so badly taught. One of the secondary aims of this project was to establish how much a practical involvement in remedial reading tuition would affect subject staffs' perceptions of learning problems in their ordinary teaching. Over this period a third of the staff had become involved in the scheme and the training programme. They came from a range of disciplines, History, English, Biology, P.E., Modern Languages and Social Studies. Some of the Mathematics staff were involved in a similar approach to Mathematics for slow learners but they, the Chemists, Physicists and Craft teachers were not included. This was partly a matter of their popularity with the low attainers, partly because of timetable difficulties and partly a result of their own career orientations. At first it seemed that those involved had begun to think more deeply about readability levels, of textbooks and worksheets on their own account. Yet the standards of the band just above the remedial group did not rise as much as we had hoped and the evidence of the third year screening tests suggested that while the 'tail' of the poor readers grew shorter, the mean stayed constant. It is arguable that if the mean had also improved, the rate of progress among the children who had had one year's remedial provision might also have done so once this was removed.

If the social psychological findings of labelling theory make criteria of success for remedial education so important, the research on its effectiveness allows one to determine them. There would seem to be little point in remedial provision, from the children's point of view, if those who have it do not make better progress than those marginally above the cut off point. This progress ought to be maintained over three years. If the model of extended remedial education is employed, the effectiveness of the information passed on to subject staff ought to be measurable in terms of the reading levels of the ability band just above the remedial group and the trends in reading progress of those for whom help has been withdrawn. The last criteria ought to be whether the children themselves are satisfied that they are getting appropriate treatment. We found that considerable progress could be made by low expectation pupils in remedial education and, as the Bullock Committee predicted, this could be ascribed to the personalities and general teaching skills of the staff rather than their knowledge of specific tests and techniques. We also found that the introduction of an effective language policy for the least able was a great deal more difficult than that committee had suggested.

Chapter Three

THE SPECIAL CLASS

Special classes for backward children in ordinary schools have a far older history than the remedial education reading and mathematics tuition groups described in the previous chapter. They seem to have emerged as a concommitant of the structural constraints of the board schools and to have been legitimated by the psychometric movement. D.H. Lawrence (1915) gives a fine account of how even the most idealistic of teachers was drawn into conflict with the slower pupils by the monotonous conformism of the standards. Ursula Brangwen's scapegoat, Williams, is described as 'a sort of defective, not bad enough to be so classed'. He resists her authority by not doing sufficient writing, distributing blots on the page, disrupting lessons and throwing tantrums. Ursula finds Williams 'sick', 'etiolated' and 'degenerate', key epithets in Lawrence's moral and aesthetic imagination which mask the political and social implications of the crisis from her and, we suspect, from the author as well. After she has caned Williams into submission, his mother comes to the school. Mrs. Williams is described in a similar way:

> ... her half beggar deportment and a sense of being unpleasant to touch, like something going bad inside. She was neither a lady nor an ordinary working man's wife, but a creature separate from society.

Teachers caught in the realities of such social confrontations and realising that the new schools for defective children were not likely to take sufficient numbers of such children from them, segregated them within the same building. Cyril Burt, whose recommendations to the Wood Committee led to official support (H.M.S.O.: 1929) for this approach, describes a school he visited shortly after the First World War where this was practised (Burt: 1937). It was in a Northern industrial area with a 'well to do working class neighbourhood' on one side and a 'poverty striken slum' on the other. On the appointment of a new headteacher:

The Special Class

> ... the eight assistants had risen in revolt; one and all had protested that good work was impossible in any of the classes, owing to the presence of two or three hopeless dunces in each room, hindering and hampering the progress of the rest. The Headmaster accordingly made a survey of the whole school. The more difficult cases were sorted out and assembled in a separate classroom with a teacher of their own. And thus was established what would nowadays be called a 'special class for difficult children', one of the earliest of its kind in the country.

The conditions of the 1944 Education Act encouraged the gradual spread of such classes which seemed especially functional when there was a large degree of psychometrically based streaming and where the political and social basis of such educational judgements were considered unproblematic. Burt's assumption of the link between social background and 'deficiency' is rooted in the attitudes of his time, though mediated by his own effusive condescension, as this description of Willie and Walter, 'sharp little Arabs of 7½', shows:

> The two little 7 year old scamps who were doing standard II work were by no means lacking in intelligence. The Headteacher had labelled them 'defective'; but he explained that by this he means morally defective, not mentally defective. They were, as he put it, criminals in the bud.

Roy Nash (1975) would conclude that where the special class is selected on the basis of teacher recommendation, similar constellations of personal and social attitudes persist in colouring educational judgements. He found that many teachers put forward the names of the children they disliked or found difficult to manage. Children from the special class were not only perceived as dull but also as 'troublesome and badly behaved' (Nash: 1975). In their review of the 'progress classes' in the Isle of Wight, Rutter, Tizard and Whitmore (1970) found very similar conditions, but then fought away from the sociological implications. In assessing the children who had been selected they found that:

> Children with reading difficulties placed in 'progress' classes in ordinary schools differed from those in ordinary classes only in relation to behaviour. (p. 143)

Even though the rationale of such classes was often seen in terms of improving reading, their function appeared to be one of containment:

> It should be emphasized that the classes may have developed for purposes other than helping children with reading difficulties. (p. 142)

What these purposes may have been and the way they fitted in with the other major functions of schools, these authors did not pursue since they no doubt would have perceived their work in epidemiological rather than sociological terms. The oversight has interesting implications, given the influence they exerted on the Warnock Committee.

Some schools round out their selection criteria with psychometric scores. These may well include group IQ tests like the N.F.E.R. Verbal Reasoning Quotient series (N.F.E.R.: 1982). Their large reading loads make them unsuitable for low ability children. A great deal of doubt has been expressed about the reliability of individual intelligence tests, also. The correlation between W.I.S.C. scores and subsequent reading progress is not high and it has been argued that the concept of IQ is itself socially and ethnically biased (Kamin: 1974, Chomsky: 1971). In her survey of Californian children referred to Educational Psychologists, Mercer (1971) found that the IQ tests were crucial in determining the entry rates of the different ethnic groups into special education classes. She found that very similar proportions of Anglo, Negro and Chicano children were thought by their parents to be mentally retarded. The teachers referred similar ratios and these were passed on by school administrators in a balanced way. The only way to account for the larger numbers of non-white children, especially Negroes, in special classes was by reference to the IQ test. Aware of this problem, Dunn (1973) calls for revisions that will take account of ethnic origins.

Other tests like those of word recognition and computational skill are also used, like Schonell (1950), the Richmond (1982) and Young tests (1969). Without reference to the child's previous interaction and syllabus these may also produce self fulfilling prophecies, as this case illustrates (Sewell: 1981). Simon had one of the poorest IQ scores and reading ages of his year and yet it was not until the end of his primary school that his mother found out that his teacher disliked him and had kept him on the same reader all year:

> If you were in this teacher's good books, that was fine. If you weren't, he didn't want to know ... So I went down when Simon was moving up to the senior school and I asked him why Simon had been kept on the same book all year and he could give no answer. He said "I've done by best. Simon's either downright lazy or stupid." I was very upset.

Having screened the year group and selected the special class, this continues either for the first three years or throughout the school. Some departments have regular case conferences and try to get some of their children into the mainstream. Because curricula often diverge, these changes are likely to be few. The main justification of a special class is to provide a special syllabus. Since the children's attainments in the 3 R's deviates so markedly from their peers, there is often a heavy concentration of work here. However, even with smaller classes, lavish resources and specially trained staff, the effects of labelling are hard to overcome. Rutter, Tizard and Whitmore (1970) concluded of the progress classes in the Isle of Wight:

> They were not successful in meeting the needs of children with specific reading retardation or with reading backwardness. (p. 143)

Unhappy though these researchers were with these effects, they did not pursue the possibility that self fulfilling prophecies might defeat all but the most indefatigable staff. This might have brought the objectivity of their epidemiological approach into question. Instead they focussed their recommendations on staff training. They set up two action research projects. The L.E.A. was first persuaded to send one teacher on a course. When she came back she was directly involved in teaching children from two secondary schools and 'advised' teachers in another two. Results were compared with two schools with "remedial streams ... where special attention was paid to their reading and two schools where no special attention was given to their disability" (p. 362). They found that the two groups taught by the trained specialist did best in terms of reading progress, but only marginally so. The groups which she 'advised' did even worse than the schools with no special provision. The results from this first project were not clear cut and the researchers set up a short in-service course for teachers of eight year olds, then compared the results with those of untrained teachers. At the end of the year, the experimental group produced scores two months higher than those of the control group, hardly a promising result, especially when there was no long term follow up. Rutter, Tizard and Whitmore claimed, however, that "the results suggest that in-service training might be of value in improving children's progress in reading during primary school".

It is interesting to compare this conclusion with the Warnock Committee's optimism about the roles of initial and in-service training courses as mechanisms for change. Enlarged teacher training provision represents one of their three 'areas of first priority'. And first in the list of 'areas in which research is needed' is:

> The updating of epidemiological studies such as the Isle of Wight Study in order to obtain information about changes in the prevalence of different handicapping conditions, including regional differences.

Whilst accepting that in-service work with teachers who are personally committed and professionally effective in relation to low status pupils may enhance their capabilities, it is possible to argue that courses which elaborate on the attributes of such pupils with less committed teachers may do more harm than good. Lacking a sociological critique, the Warnock Committee appears to treat concepts such as 'prevalence' as value free. Yet as Rutter, Tizard and Whitmore unwittingly demonstrate, they may well generate self fulfilling prophecies. Defining children as backward in order to locate candidates for special classes may help to perpetuate low attainments. Providing teachers who do not identify with such children with an uncritical training in the assessment of 'needs' could thereby legitimate such labelling processes.

This has critical implications for Warnock's conception of the special class as a 'resource room'. Lacking a serious consideration of the ambiguities of labelling, the Warnock Committee offers special education an 'a priori' rationale, based on the differentiation between the aims and objectives of education. The aims of education are thought to be the same for all children. They are subdivided into the intrinsic and the instrumental:

> They are first to enlarge a child's knowledge, experience and imaginative understanding and thus his awareness of moral values and capacity for enjoyment; and secondly to enable him to enter the world after formal education is over as an active participant in society and a responsible contributor to it, capable of achieving as much independence as possible.

Given that all children have needs in order to move towards such goals, then the greater difficulties of the physically handicapped child and the backward reader entitle them to special consideration. The existence of special needs, quantified through epidemiological concepts like prevalence, helps explain differences in terms of objectives. Whereas examination courses leading to CSE or 'O' level are seen as realistic for the majority of children, they are clearly beyond the reach of the slow learner. That is not to say that it is not worthwhile including such children in our understanding of education. Indeed, unless the objectives of the minority are clearly spelt out and regularly re-evaluated, the Warnock Committee feels that the groups of children for whom special classes and resource rooms are intended are less likely to progress towards these aims. Hence there is a trend, encouraged by their report for special schools, units and classes, to move towards a greater specification of individualized objectives and syllabus content.

The Committee recommended that all children with special educational needs ought to have full individual records and regular reviews, whether they attended ordinary or special schools. This might have made it possible to monitor and hence improve teaching standards. This seems to have been the main aim in America. There, however, parental access to school records is more of an issue. The passing of Public Law

PL 94-142 has allowed the parents of handicapped children to have regular reviews of progress. It is arguable though that without such safeguards, critical self assessment of teachers becomes more of a pipe dream. The 1981 Education Act left the evaluation of the progress of children in ordinary schools, about whom no statement is required, to the discretion of the headteacher.

If this fails to bring any more effective pressure on the teachers, it is not impossible for a tightly structured objectives programme to translate low teacher expectations into curricula which continue to constrict pupil progress. In a comparative study of nine East Midlands ESN schools and five secondary schools, Geoff Davies (1981) found the provision of objectives programmes had had no obvious benefits for pupils. There was insufficient time for him to engage in a full scale evaluation of the range of teaching and administrative approaches, but he concludes:

> It was particularly disappointing that the comparisons with the results of earlier studies demonstrated that at least this sample shows no sign of improvement, although over recent years there has been an expansion of special educational provision, increased production of materials and teaching methods and a greater provision of in-service teacher training.

Contrary to the presuppositions of the Warnock Committee, it may be possible for subject staff in ordinary schools to produce stimulating and effective learning experiences for low status children without articulating specific objectives for them. Where teachers have high expectations and the children are willing to take risks and engage in new areas of interest, segregation in a resource room or special class could well be minimised. This is particularly true of children when they first arrive at secondary school. Some low expectation pupils do find this a stressful period, but many teachers are at their most sympathetic with first year pupils, possibly as this first year pastoral tutor suggests, they are least threatened by them (Sewell: 1981):

> Especially in the first year, children who are in need of a great deal of help like that generally get as much as we can give. Usually they are eager to better themselves and improve their standards and staff go along with this.

Where special classes exist in the lower forms of the comprehensive schools, and their teachers are aware that their own teaching in some of the subject areas is "sometimes limited in scope and in the challenge which it presents to individuals" (Warnock: para. 11:1), there has been a trend for them to establish links with other departments. They may simply be asked to help prepare curricular objectives, or especially sympathetic and reliable staff may be invited to teach the special class. In contact with the full range of ability, these teachers may help some of the special class pupils to question some of their low self-expectations.

For teachers and pupils alike, the problems become much more acute in the last two years of school. Even with a complex option system, it is not always possible to place children with teachers who can present a lively and appropriate syllabus or include them in work that is aimed at the rest of the class and their examinations. Just as the elementary school teachers of Edwardian England found the demands of the standards polarized the class and intensified the pressures towards discipline and conformity, so upper school teachers find themselves battling with low expectation pupils and presenting them with work they know to be 'unreal' and 'irrelevant' (Brennan: 1979). The Bullock Report suggests that a support option be set up for fourth and fifth year pupils who had weaknesses in language skills. This would also extend the pastoral work of the school and help the pupils become less alienated.

Where special classes are set up for a limited proportion of the upper school timetable, it is easy for staff to feel that they are merely calming pupils after other teachers' confrontations. In the children's best interests a more extensive programme is needed and a more coherent policy established. The special classes could cater for different individuals for varying lengths of time, providing a sanctuary for those who cannot cope with mainstream work or who cannot be coped with by any other staff, but also allowing pupils to work for examinations in options they care for and make progress in. The emphasis would again be on extending basic skills, but often rather within the context of a 'life skills' or 'integrated studies' course rather than as separate reading, spelling and arithmetic lessons. Hence computational skills may well be reinforced through social mathematics. Problems that have to be faced in adult life, like budgeting, paying for gas, electricity, making hire purchase agreements on motor bikes and furniture, act as starting points for lessons.

There have been many attempts to put such life skills programmes on an objectives basis and by far the most extended of these, which grew out of the experience of a number of American special class teachers, was written up by Kolstoe (1972). The curriculum is divided into ten broad areas. Pupils in their last few years at school are encouraged to think in terms of vocational and leisure skills. Each age group is given a series of behaviouristically defined goals. Under the heading of hygiene, school leavers are expected to know how to bandage a wound and verbalize the dangers of contagious disease. In safety, they should be able to fill out an accident form, for instance. There are three major criticisms one could make of an objectives approach to life skills programme which this book exemplified. Firstly it emphasizes

Life skills

verbal accountability at the cost of concrete experience. Secondly it makes separate skills out of what could be quite appropriately learned through sensitive pupil-teacher interaction and thirdly it equates successful learning with a middle class view of the world.

A few illustrations could make these issues clearer. In the group of objectives concerned with geography and finding one's way about, children at the 'intermediate' level are asked to describe how they would get home using bus or subway; at 'prevocational' level to name major geographical regions; at the 'vocational' level to find the points of a compass and produce routes using one. There are quite a few children in the fourth and fifth years of British comprehensive schools who would find it difficult to explain how to find one's way home using public transport, or to produce a traffic route for themselves. In some cases, this may well be because they have never had to. Put in a situation like planning the route for a class trip or finding their way home from one, they might learn this much more easily than in a class lesson.

Kolstoe's list of objectives at least reminds the teacher of what children ought to know in a clear and simple manner. Yet it over-simplifies the more complex issues of social interaction. One of the objectives is: if a pupil is in a disagreement with another person, he ought to be able to accept the situation 'as evidenced by his willingness to talk to or work with the other person'. There are children who, put in situations of confrontation in school, may not be able to talk themselves out of it. They lack survival skills for school which may well have considerable value outside as well. Yet starting work in a factory the ex-pupil may well be given unpleasant jobs and bullied. It may only be by standing up for himself that he gains others' respect. This is not always done by showing willingness 'to talk or work with that other person'.

Low expectation pupils may well know more about appropriate behaviour in stressful work situations than their teachers. One of the author's ex-pupils was working with a foreman who teased him and made unwelcome sexual advances. Keith was angry, swore at the man and told him what he thought of him. His teachers would not have been surprised to hear that Keith had lost his job for swearing at the foreman. In fact he kept it. Despite the evidence that many ex-pupils from special class lose jobs because of poor factory discipline (Chaffin et al: 1971), it may also be true that in difficult conditions one can be too polite. An approach to the ethics of life skills which allows pupils and teachers to learn from each others' experiences may be more appropriate, impossible though this would be to reduce to a programme of behavioural objectives.

Life skill approaches may result in curricula that are banal and undemanding for pupils as well as teachers. Lessons about the appropriate behaviour of adult life could as well be learned through the medium of social studies, History or drama.

The Special Class

Many special classes for slow learners in this country study local history and geography, moving beyond the here and now to a sense of the environment and how it came to be. A mathematics project about budgeting can grow, as Midwinter (1971) has shown, into a comparative survey of local prices, involving concepts like averages and percentages, as well as technical skills like using calculators and personal skills like interviewing shopkeepers. Many of those concerned with low attainers stop short at such descriptive activities as if this was the greatest educational advance the children were capable of making. However, as more and more specialist Geography teachers are realizing, their subject is about values. Analysing phenomena in terms of values can be a stimulating and worthwhile geographical exercise, particularly where these phenomena impinge on the pupils' own lives.

Having collected and tabulated their data about shop prices, the pupils can then be invited to reflect on why there should be such differences. The pupils themselves might know how this reflects labour intensiveness and patterns of ownership. Notions of wage structures can then be pursued through topics like unionism and the role of the unemployed in a competitive economy. These are hard lessons for pupils who have so much to fear from recession yet, handled in an exploratory way, through pupil centred discussion, it can lead to exciting and relevant debate. It has the advantage of treating them as intelligent young adults with an interest in what happens to them. It involves them in the realities of post school life, whilst breathing new life into the traditional academic disciplines. Whilst it may be argued that a lively discussion on unemployment may generate the same sort of despair as we earlier suggested could derive from poor teaching and inappropriate discipline, the author has found that the reverse is true. This is an area of great risks and uncertainties, however, and while no answers may be found, it may be as well for special class teachers to share their concerns with other subject specialists or the careers staff.

Similar issues can be reached through the teaching of an historical period or theme. Many teachers of history are sceptical of the traditional approach with its emphasis on the reiteration of historical facts and dates. They would prefer to offer children primary evidence which must first be brought to life imaginatively then subjected to inferential and critical analysis and lastly translated into other media. There are undeniable difficulties for the slow learner even in the more recent approaches to history. Some of the evidence offered, like that included in Jackdaw packs (Jackdaw: 1970), have readability levels that are too high and grammatical patterns that are unfamiliar to poor readers. Though often willing to speculate, many low expectation pupils find that trying to do this within the terms of textual constraints quite frustrating. It has even been suggested that the levels of abstraction appropriate to perceiving a period in the light of its own value system is beyond all but the most gifted adolescents (Hallam: 1971).

Nevertheless, the least able may be able to perceive links between events and attitudes that coexisted in a different period, where a discussion or imaginative recreation has brought each to life sufficiently. The author involved one non-examination group in a topic about working class life between the wars. They read parts of Love on the Dole, Borstal Boy and other contemporary materials which were within their reading abilities. They discussed the material and its social, personal and political implications, re-enacted certain scenes through improvised drama and wrote essays and stories about it. They were able to understand apprenticeship schemes and how they could be exploited in times of recession. They explored the I.R.A. campaign and prison life in the 1930's and they made some sense of the sexual 'mores' of the time. They were also able to make fleeting connections between these separate topics.

One lesson became so real that it burst through the constraints of the author's teaching objectives. The topic was strikes. The Callaghan government was currently facing its 'winter of discontent'. Some of the pupils' parents had taken part in one of the most significant industrial disputes of this time, so they knew about picket lines, losing pay and union negotiation. I had brought in some material from the 1930's which we started to read in a half hearted sort of way. One of them then said "We don't want to read about strikes. We want to have one." There ensued a scriptless drama lesson whose outcome no-one could have foretold. We negotiated in a disorganized sort of way. They could not agree terms between themselves so the negotiations broke down. A strike committee was set up and shop stewards elected. They now had some machinery for determining things among themselves and I was asked to leave the room. The shop stewards then came and negotiated with me. I got them to concede things they had no brief from the committee to do and when they returned the committee sacked them. After three quarters of an hour I brought in two members of staff who knew the pupils and were interested in the class, to arbitrate. The discussion turned to the broader issues of the futility of their coming to school, school conditions, school meals and so on. Eventually it was agreed that if they were to continue working hard until the end of the fifth year, there would have to be a proper rate for the job.

As improvisation and an introduction to practical politics, this lesson was extremely useful. The pupils had to call upon resources of general knowledge and logical thinking which hardly ever seemed to exist in school. It satisfied a few of the 'Educational Objectives for the Study of History' as defined by Coltham and Fines (1971). These were, for instance, oral and reading comprehension skills, translation of material from one medium - print - into another - drama, analytical skills in spotting bias in me and balance in the arbitrator, inferential skills in working out how far their shop stewards had been misled by management, vocabulary acquisition, memorization and of course empathetic identification (Hull: 1979). Yet, in terms of their grounding these skills in a understanding of the past, the lesson appeared at the time to have been a failure. Their own experiences and needs had crowded into the picture, robbing them of historical detachment. It was only in retrospect, and then only in partial and confused ways, that they could relate this experience to the exercises we have previously done about the 1930's policy of taking on school leavers as apprentices, then sacking them when they had served their apprenticeship. In order to get the best out of those pupils in that lesson we had to suspend the forms of knowledge associated with history.

This approach to special class teaching had three major elements. The first could be defined as a concern for relationships, such that cues about pupil interests and unsuspected intellectual potential could be followed up as they emerged. The second was a concern for the development of clear and purposeful thinking, mainly through the medium of spoken language. There had been a breakdown in the formal structure of the lesson. This was a real problem which the pupils had to help me to solve. The third element comes relatively close to the definition of a liberal education as Hirst (1972) saw it in relation to an objectives approach:

> In the first place, as liberal education is concerned with the comprehensive development of the mind in acquiring knowledge, it is aimed at achieving an understanding of experience in many different ways. This means the acquisition by critical training and discipline not only of facts but also of complex conceptual schemes and of the arts and techniques of different types of reasoning and judgement. Syllabuses and curricula cannot therefore be constructed simply in terms of information and isolated skills. They must be constructed so as to introduce pupils as far as possible into the inter-related aspects of each of the basic forms of knowledge, each of the several disciplines. And they must be constructed to cover at least in some measure the range of knowledge as a whole.

Hirst has criticised schools for failing to provide a common curriculum: "(there are) no adequate grounds for saying this is impossible when we have in fact spent so little of our effort trying to achieve this" (Hirst: 1969). Hard pressed teachers of alienated fourth and fifth year pupils may well find such remarks hypocritical when they issue from the safety of a University Education Department. Yet it is precisely when pupils see so little meaning in school that the teacher has to question an approach which rests at the acquisition of facts and isolated skills. Intelligent and appropriate behaviour, especially when it means testing out the forms of knowledge in relation to their own experience, may well bring them into a more participatory role. When the relationship is strong enough, a small special class can also allow the teacher to get the pupils to test out their own 'conceptual schemes' in terms of 'different types of reasoning and judgement'.

These are the central issues in the relationship between the special class and the teacher of science. Many science specialists seem to find it difficult to translate their ideas into words that low expectation students can understand. Barnes (1969) quotes this example of a teacher who seems to want to avoid using the term 'under reflux conditions' but finds the linguistic conventions so strong that he ends up misusing it:

> If we did it using a different method actually .. where we heat up the grass with acetone actually .. heating it under .. er .. an enclosed system except .. I'll have to show using a diagram on that .. well, er .. under reflux conditions so that we didn't lose the acetone then we could actually finish up with the grass a white colour.

In the same lesson the teacher invites the class to speculate and when a pupil produces the wrong answer the teacher codes this as if it were a slip of the tongue rather than what seems to be in the context of the lesson a serious misconception:

> T. Now I don't know whether any of you could jump the gun a bit and tell me what actually is this green stuff which produces green colour ..
> P. Er .. um .. water.
> T. No .. Have you heard of chlorophyll?

Pupils may find it almost impossible to grasp certain scientific concepts when presented in an abstract form and in conventional terminology. Allowed to use their own language and intuitive thinking, as in this illustration by Sutton (1974), they may be able to progress much further:

> Theresa: I think .. em .. there might be more source in the centre - more source of power - or more ..
> Teacher: So you think the marble chips aren't the same all the way through, then?
> Theresa: No it's not that, only .. em .. I think that .. that once you've chopped it up there's no .. em .. what can I say?
> Elaine: (chipping in) You get to the inside quicker.

The Newsom Report (H.M.S.O.: 1963, para. 440) regarded the relationship of terminology, scientific concepts and limited ability in these terms:

> It would be comparatively easy to go through an interesting and useful course without dwelling on the great unifying concepts - the energy chain, evolution, the balance of nature, the simpler quantitative laws (perhaps understood pictorially) and the like. They may be beyond some pupils but those who have any chance of grasping them, even apparently fleetingly, should have the opportunity.

Helpful and practical though these suggestions are, they neglect what the teacher concerned with what Hirst referred to as the development of mind. In a small special class it may be possible to pick up limitations in pupil thinking then attempt to overcome them through reference to forms of knowledge such as science. This is not easily done and it requires a strong relationship, an ability to use a wide linguistic register and an understanding of the subject. One of the author's groups drew a picture of the human eyeball, supposedly from a plastic model, during a science lesson. At the back of the retina there was a strange shaped blob. When asked what this was, Sarah said "It's a tree, isn't it?" I did not know what she meant, so I asked her why she had put a tree there. There was a further exchange, during which Sarah became tense and angry. Eventually another of the group said that in the second year they had had to copy a diagram of an eyeball from a textbook in which the eye was 'looking' at a tree. The blob at the back of the eyeball was the inverted image of the tree. Sarah got upset because she felt she had been 'shown up'. I could not understand why she should have remembered this aspect of the original exercise, even though she had forgotten its purpose, as well as the underlying concept. The incident degenerated into a disciplinary issue and Sarah retained her imperfect conceptual schema.

With another group, a similar misunderstanding occurred, but the outcome was more positive. We had just finished making a cine film and were splicing and editing. The narrative of the film was in three parts, but it had only been shot in two locations. The first scene was shot in school, the second outside, the third back in school again. As a commercial film maker would have done, we made the first and last scenes on the same day. The plot of the film had been made up by the special class and they ought all to have understood the shooting sequence. One boy, Clifford, asked why we had to stick the middle bit of film at the end. As in Sarah's case, the boy's assumptions were so alien to mine that I simply did not know what he meant. I simply said, in terms that made ample sense to me, though not to him, that we had shot the last part of the story in the middle. He replied that when his father used his cine camera, he just shot the film and 'showed it as it was'. This suggested that Clifford supposed that a film was a reflection of reality, much like a mirror was. It was as difficult for him to understand that one can transpose film images as it would have been for a scientist to think of peeling reflections from a mirror. At a cognitive level, it seemed that taking events out of their temporal flow in order to create new meanings represented an understanding of time whose abstractness defeated Clifford. He was just aware, however, that his stock of knowledge was qualitatively different from mine and that this was a topic he wanted to learn about.

The best way for me to teach him was to reduce an abstract problem to concrete examples. We examined the film itself and talked about the way it was composed of a series of still frames. We discussed the way that running static images in front of the eye gave the illusion of movement - as when a series of faces are drawn at the corner of a book and then allowed to flicker past very fast. We looked at a projector and showed how the shutter mechanism allowed each frame to be shown very briefly and then replaced by another. Just as in a comic book you could change the faces on the corner of the pages to produce a flickering movement. So, by editing the film and putting parts of it in a different order you could change the illusion to suit yourself. The film itself was not the original event. The camera had just made pictures of that event that could be used to tell a story.

Using the Socratic method, I then asked Clifford to say whether there were any films he watched that he thought were real but that he knew were not. At that point he realized that when adults said that 'Starsky and Hutch' was 'only a film', this must be exactly what they had meant. That realization represented a gestalt, an irreversible and qualitative change in his thinking about films and television. If a film had to be shot and edited, it meant that it was quite different from the picture he saw when he looked out of a window or through a telescope. You did not have to believe what you saw. You could even criticise it as being unlifelike or unbelievable. I then asked him if there was anything most people believed on television, but which he now knew must have been made up in exactly this way. He said, 'The news'.

In shooting the film and talking about it, the group surprised myself and themselves by their zest and the fertility of their imaginations. Getting out of the classroom was a way of breaking expectations. The boys wrote the script themselves. Trouble in lessons was followed by a morning in the woods and eventual retribution. They were constantly making suggestions about how to make the film, what role each other should play, what details to put in to keep up the vitality. Where many of their other lessons seemed time filling and demoralising, this filled them with creative energy and restored their curiosity. Like Sarah in the 'sight' lesson, Clifford had found difficulty in managing a concept out of a familiar context. His readiness to attempt this followed from his willingness to accept the possibility of a mistake. Mistakes, ignorance and stupidity have, in contexts like these, far reaching personal and social implications. These are daily compounded by an atmosphere of mistrust and mental lethargy. In order to overcome all this, there has firstly to be an assurance that neither teacher nor class will 'show a pupil up' (Woods: 1979). Secondly, there has to be a preparedness on the teacher's part to extend partial concepts whose meaning to the child might be quite different to the teacher's. Thirdly, there has to be a facility with language and ideas such that the teacher can communicate with the pupil about these partial concepts as they arise.

The Warnock Report makes plain that special education does not merely exist in special schools, units or classes, but then argues that it is to be defined as that which provides for special needs. This in turn could be assessed in terms of achievement relative to certain educational objectives. If one argued that successful teaching is not to be evaluated merely in terms of product, but that processes of developing understanding were at least as important, then one could redefine special education in broader and more positive terms. The processual paradigm would focus on the fruitfulness of the cognitive and interactional exchanges and on the sensitivity of the teacher to possibilities as well as deficiencies. The objectives approach, stimulating though it is proving to curricular considerations for low expectation pupils, may well prove as one-sided for successful special class teaching as the pupil centred philosophy it seeks to replace. It seems to close off teacher serendipity, the ability to gather on a moment to moment basis what children might be capable of. The child centred approach, for its part, may well have led to learning that was disorganized and superficial. The special education teacher probably needs to conduct a dialogue between his own sense of goals and the pupils' curiosity, skilfully blending both strategies.

This processual paradigm of special education would also suggest that it cannot be confined to special classes. It may be that calling a group of children the special class makes it even more difficult to bring about. James Herndon gives an illustration of such a class he taught mathematics (Beck et al: 1975). Inside the classroom they considered themselves the 'Dumb Class' and there was little Herndon could do to overcome their lack of intellectual confidence. He took some of them out to a bowling alley one night and met some of the weakest in his group keeping score. What they were doing was more difficult than they would do in school. As most special class teachers would, he jotted down some examples of scoring problems and took them into school next day:

> I figured I had this particular dumb kid now. Back in eighth period I lectured him on how smart he was to be a league scorer in bowling. I pried admissions from the other boys about how they had paper routes and made change. I made the girls confess that when they went to buy stuff they didn't have any difficulty deciding if those shoes cost $10.95 or whether it meant $109.50 or whether it meant $1.09

> or how much change they'd get back from twenty. Naturally I then handed out bowling score problems and buying shoe problems and naturally everyone could choose which ones they wanted to solve and naturally the result was that all the dumb kids immediately rushed me yelling: Is this right? I don't know how to do it! What's the answer? This ain't right, is it? and What's my grade? The girls who bought shoes for $10.95 with a $20 bill came up with $400.15 for change and wanted to know if that was right. The brilliant league scorer couldn't decide whether two strikes and a third frame of eight amounted to eighteen or twenty eight or whether it was one hundred, eight and one half.

Special class teachers see the same kind of self-distrust congealing in their class as their reputation for bad behaviour grows. One day I was unable to take Clifford and Sam's group and they were posted to another member of staff. There was a misunderstanding and he also had other commitments. The class, however, had thought he had said "I am not taking Geof's group" and they had scattered throughout the school. Making up a special class in the upper school like that renders them all the more notorious and one then has to judge whether the advantages really outweigh the drawbacks. In one school the remedial staff might feel that it is better to concentrate the least able and most difficult in a special class. In another, where the staff resources are different, it might be possible to rely on a federation of especially able staff to take options with different but overlapping groups. Where the children are likely to be concentrated - bottom English and Mathematics sets, Social Studies, General Science and Child Care options - and where these are taught by the minority of teachers which Brophy and Good refer to, it may be possible to dispense with a permanent special class.

Since there is so little guarantee that a non-examination special class will be in its pupils' best interests, it is all the more important that the special teacher should make himself accountable. Criteria for success ought to include an improvement in reading standards. Direct instruction in reading often finishes at the third year in comprehensive schools. The explanation for this is either that if a child has still failed to read by then he will not improve in the last two years, or that the adult literacy schemes will always be there to help after he has left. The success of these schemes ought to have convinced remedial teachers that the context and relationship matter more than the client's age. It may well be true that older pupils resent going back over books and materials they used in the lower school, in which case they must have different approaches and new books. These can often be borrowed from the schools' library service. Play reading and silent reading can be emphasized for those with reasonable primary and intermediate skills, but where children have substantial difficulties, individual tuition with especially trusted staff may have to be organized.

Other aspects of the curriculum could well be evaluated on the lines that Warnock and Brennan (1979) suggest. Is the curriculum as challenging and as wide in scope as that available to peers, or does a special class mean there is over-simplified science and history, or worse still, none at all? Would it hlep to set down goals and objectives and to carry out evaluations and curricular reviews? In his "Curricular Needs of Slow Learners" (1979) Brennan takes rather a one-sided line, arguing that where these are implicit and dependant on informal liaison, the curriculum suffers:

> Some small special and promary schools, along with some secondary departments, devoted considerable time to discussion of the curriculum and held the view that the intimacy and quality of communication made written curricula unnecessary. There were good, successful schools among them, but the success often rested on the quality of teaching and organization rather than the curriculum. It is asking a great deal of any individual teacher or group of teachers to keep in mind all aspects of the curriculum required for the task of arranging regular revision and review.

Our redefinition of special education in terms of teacher-pupil relationships, the quality of teaching and the teachers' use of "the inter-related aspects of each of the basic forms of knowledge" (Hirst: op cit: 1971) in order to enhance the development of mind, render Brennan's distinctions between curriculum and teaching spurious. As Brennan himself admits, it is quite possible to have promising written curricula and poor teaching. Indeed many schools, successful and unsuccessful, are now using Nuffield approaches in the teaching of science. Yet only one in six were doing so satisfactorily in the view of his report. Our rather more process orientated view of special education, with its dialogue between the teacher's sense of goals and the pupils' emerging curiosity, would lead us to stress the importance of attaining sufficiently high levels of communication among staff. The other major difficulty in applying an objectives model of the curriculum to comprehensive school teaching is that while heads of departments can be invited to write curricula, there is insufficient power to enforce their effective application.

Davies's previously mentioned study includes information about one ESN(M) school whose objectives approach to the curriculum was for a time nationally known. The author visited the school to make a study of the effectiveness of its language teaching. All the children in the school had an oral language lesson with tape recorders and a written comprehension every morning. Control was extraordinarily tight and in the reception class, teacher talk took an average of ninety per cent of teacher-pupil interaction, measured using the Flanders Amydon interaction analysis (Morrison and McIntyre: 1972). With the school leavers' class, the proportion had fallen to seventy per cent. Analysis of the utterances of the oldest children, noted in lessons and at breaktimes, showed poorly developed syntactical structures which rarely included qualifiers and were brief. By chance, the author had an opportunity to observe children from the neighbouring ESN(S) school who were being considered for transfer. Several of these children used larger, more sophisticated sentences, judging from their formal lesson responses and their informal lunchtime conversations. It was possible to conduct the same sort of interaction analysis and this showed a higher proportion of teacher time reflecting and amplifying pupil speech. In this case, the staff had developed a strong link with the speech therapist. She had brought in her notes on language development from college and explained the basic principles in terms of the children within that school. She had shown them how to conduct an assessment of children's language and the teachers felt that this had helped them to understand what they were supposed to be doing.

The issues involved in the assessment of language development programmes are extremely complex and it may well have been that the children with well developed language in the ESN(S) school might have been placed there because of inordinate difficulties in other areas. The fact that one objectives approach allowed little opportunity for pupil-teacher interaction cannot be used to criticise the strategy itself. Yet there is a problem involved which Stake (1967) and other curriculum evaluators (e.g. Hamilton et al: 1977) have explored but which the Warnock Report and Brennan have not. It may be that for all the detail involved in a programme of educational objectives, there may be a series of contingencies which impede pupil progress towards them. These contingencies may well add up to what has been referred to as 'hidden curriculum'. The teachers may not be as conscious of this as of their overt objectives, yet their common sense and intuition may tell them that it is bad for teacher control to allow too much pupil talk, for instance. Seeing themselves as constructors of a programme, they fail to take the wider view. They do not question the lack of 'congruence' between stated goals and actual achievement or the degree of congruence between their control mechanisms and pupil behaviour. These are no longer as relevant to their view of themselves as teachers. In this case, well educated and autonomous professionals might well be more successful than those following objectives approaches. Where teachers are well motivated, as they appeared to be in both the ESN(M) and ESN(S) schools, it may be asking too little of them <u>not</u> to "keep in mind all aspects of the curriculum required for the task of arranging regular revision and review" (Brennan: op cit).

The crucial problem in evaluation of who monitors the teachers remains. Those who favour objectives approaches would suggest that teachers can best review their own attainments. If only the objectives could be specified clearly enough, the teachers merely have to apply criteria referenced tests to the pupils. Brennan admits, however, that special schools, especially residential schools which have little contact with mainstream educational standards, risk lowering their expectations unwittingly. The American experience would suggest that an important guarantee of appropriate curricula for mainstreamed handicapped pupils is to make funding dependent on regular parent-teacher reviews. In this country, where we do not have the same pattern of state and parental intervention, an alternative for the special class teacher is to ask the parents and children themselves. This may be done on a regular and informal basis, term by term, asking for comments on the curriculum and suggestions for improvements. Some schools in Britain have invited pupils to make out reports on their own achievements and the teachers' at the same time as the official reports are sent to parents. Many take this exercise extremely seriously and although the remarks are often humorously phrased, they can be studied and incisive. When parents are seen, they too can be asked to pass their own comments on the education their children are getting. On a large term basis, ex-special class pupils can be invited back to talk over with teachers and present pupils what they found useful in retrospect, what was interesting in its own right and what deserves to be changed. On one very useful and rather formal occasion, an ex-pupil who had very nearly been excluded on several occasions led an assembly with me, answering questions about how he'd got a job, how he had been able to stand up to the older men's banter and how he now ran an assembly line with some of these older men working for him. He talked about the trouble he had been in at school and his difficulties with the police, but he kept stressing the importance of never giving way to a lack of confidence in yourself and always trying to think intelligently in difficult situations. This in turn could be related to his experience of school and what certain of the teachers had taught him through the medium of their subjects.

Examination success ought also to play a part in this evaluation exercise. It is not impossible for children previously ascertained ESN or others with reading ages less than nine and a half to pass CSE, provided they are well motivated and have sufficiently skilled teachers. For most low expectation pupils, these passes will often be in practical subjects, but the author has known a few passing English and limited grade Arithmetic. The special class teacher has to decide with the child how worthwhile this is, considering the local significance of a Grade 4 or 5 pass for employers and the nature of the course. Some pupils may start a CSE literature course, able with the teacher's help and support to write a reasonably clear precis of a book or story and add a few critical comments of their own, yet the prevalence of copying notes from textbooks and of the belief that simply covering paper with words constitutes work makes them impatient with the intellectual challenge. The CSE folder may then degenerate into a series of excerpts assembled from the books with little understanding or critical insight. Pupils put in for CSE plumbing might learn a great deal of practical use through a well constructed programme of objectives, although this exercise too can result in a collection of partial concepts hastily instilled to create the right impression on the day.

It may well be that the pupil himself feels the CSE is irrelevant, in which case an alternative examination, possibly taken from the City and Guilds Foundation course, may offer more scope. Chosen with care, these courses can be quite stimulating and the general prestige of the examination might be higher than that of a CSE grade 5 anyway. Some special classes give their ex-pupils certificates which they can then decide whether to use or not, as they go to Youth Employment. A refinement on this, which has the added advantage of motivating a wide range of pupil centred written activities, is the Record of Personal Achievement. Some Swindon teachers found that if the pupils were given a book with a hard cover and a set of cards inside divided into topics they could get children who would otherwise resent being shown up in front of teachers to write to a high standard, provided the book was seen as private and their own property. The Schools Council evaluation of this scheme (Swales: 1979) stressed that while this form of continuous pupil-centred assessment was far more relevant than that offered by formal examinations, it did not impress employers, even when they had been previously briefed. There would appear to be little way of getting round the underlying political and economic problem. In a society where schools play a large part in determining employment status, no examination system is going to show low expectation pupils in a good light. In redefining academic success in pupil-centred terms, as RPA seeks to do, it has a positive effect on morale. Yet, as ex-pupils find, it also encourages employers to think that they could not even have passed CSE.

A further aspect of the evaluation exercise must be the social and emotional development of the child. How does he see himself in relation to children whom the school defines as 'CSE', 'O levels', 'high fliers' and so on? Does the special class image exacerbate difficulties? Sociograms have been used to establish group boundaries and social isolates. It is interesting that Hargreaves's pioneer study (1967) of peer group formation in a secondary school excluded the bottom set:

> ... not only because of their severe difficulties in answering questionnaires without individual attention, but also because they tended to form a separate group in terms of friendship choices and special teachers assigned to them.

It may have been an oversight that evidence of the mechanisms of this social isolation was not included in the book. Teachers armed with more informal methods of participant observation might also feel ethical objections about Hargreaves' methods. Adolescents often dislike the idea of teachers tabulating friendship groups on the basis of their written preferences. There ought to be a range of other cues. In taking away groups of children for the weekend, is the special class teacher asked for friends outside the class to be invited? If so, which children want to join? In after school and community activities, do the special class join the same clubs or go to the same discos as other pupils? Sensitivity to peer relationships might be more significant than factual evidence, anyway.

Where special classes exist and are considered as the basis for resource rooms for the integration of children from special schools, it must be remembered that there are subject and primary school staff who are just as capable of providing the right 'milieux'. Jamieson, Parlett and Pocklington (1977) thought that this social psychological dimension was more significant than the personal attributes of the children or the educational hardware available. In a school where there were sufficient members of staff who could be relied upon to overcome the lowest pupil expectations, there might be all the more reason to hope for full integration. In that case the role of the special class teacher is to be more than a teacher of children with special needs. They must also monitor, facilitate and co-ordinate the work of a range of other teachers.

Chapter Four

THE CO-ORDINATION OF SPECIAL EDUCATION

The Warnock Committee was plainly unhappy about the term 'Remedial Education'. We have argued that from the social psychological perspective, their interpretation of special provision for children in ordinary schools differs little from the traditions of Burt and Schonell:

> Children in these so-called 'remedial' groups have a wide variety of individual needs, sometimes linked to psychological or physical factors, which call for skilled and discriminating attention by the staff - in assessment, the devising of suitable programmes and the organization of group or individual teaching, whether in ordinary or special classes.

They reasoned that children receiving 'remedial treatment' included those:

> who have been absent from school and need to make up work which they have missed; children with physical or sensory difficulties, sometimes temporary, sometimes permanent; children with varying degrees of learning difficulties and children who need to be temporarily withdrawn from the normal class for specific purposes.

If disabilities are permanent, there is little that can be done to 'remedy' them. The term itself suggests:

> that these children have something wrong with them that can be put right. It is true that some of them are suffering only a temporary learning difficulty and given appropriate help are able to return rapidly to their previous classes, having completely overcome their disability.

Whilst accepting that previous definitions of remedial education were both too narrow and over optimistic, we would have to question some of the basic assumptions of this paragraph (3.39). As Collins (1961) and subsequent researchers found, there is little guarantee that overcoming what seems to have been a temporary learning difficulty has much long term effect. The labelling effect in itself renders the provision of special education inappropriate in certain cases, whilst in other cases where there has been no special provision children may recover spontaneously (Cashdan, Pumfrey and Lunzer: 1971). There are even greater difficulties in arguing, as Warnock does, that those who do not respond to such provision 'require special help and support throughout their school lives'. It is only in terms of overcoming the lowest teacher/pupil expectations that special educational provision retains any meaning. This may take place, as the Warnock Committee suggested of remedial education, either in 'ordinary or special classes'.

One may suppose that in making such distinctions, the Warnock Committee wished to retain those between 'slow learners' and pupils with 'specific learning difficulties in reading, writing and spelling'. The slow learner could be defined as a child whose reading and writing attainments could be predicted by his poor IQ score. The pupil with specific learning difficulties might have an IQ score at any point on the IQ range, but his reading score was at some predefined point below that predicted on the basis of the child's age and IQ. Rutter, Tizard and Whitmore adopted the criteria of two Standard Deviations and a short W.I.S.C. score in their epidemiological study of the Isle of Wight. Using multiple regression techniques on these data, Yule and Rutter (1976) claimed to have found a larger proportion of such discrepancies than could be explained in terms of standard error. Tansley and Panckhurst (1981) argue that these statistics provide important evidence for the existence of a pathological group which could have been defined as 'dyslexic', except that such a term implies constitutional origins. The evidence of organic brain defects is slight, however, and the actual statistical discrepancy on the original data is only of the order of 1.2 per cent. In most cases reading attainments were so poor that the children fell below the absolute cut off point prescribed for remedial treatment.

If the labelling process that attends remedial and special class formation undermines the work that it aims to effect, one alternative for the poor reader of high or low IQ might be to make the provision voluntary. If a pupil had difficulty with work, whether caused by absence, lack of understanding or more generalized reading, spelling or handwriting problems, his teacher might invite him to spend a short but intensive period with the remedial teacher. Working in good surroundings with very small groups, this generalist teacher would attempt to diagnose the root of the problem and prescribe an individual programme. The pupil might furthermore be encouraged to take out a contract with the teacher to reach specified educational goals in a given period of time. Because there is a limit to the period of segregation and because if has a specific purpose, motivation can be expected to be higher. Because attendance is voluntary the negative effects of labelling ought to be ameliorated. Sixth formers with spelling problems work alongside alienated fourth formers and first year backward readers.

Examples of such an approach to remedial education can be cited in the literature (e.g. Galletley: 1975) although they tend to be rare in practice (Wilcox and Eustace: 1980). The obvious criteria for success would be: firstly whether intervention was tested and positively evaluated in the short and long term and secondly whether the clients themselves were satisfied. Unfortunately there are no instances of formal evaluation. The obvious weakness of such an approach is that some of the pupils with serious learning difficulties who might have benefitted with skilled and sympathetic teaching might be disregarded. Those who had this would only do so for short periods. It may well be that there are many children who make rapid strides in the learning of a subject or a skill in the short term, but the research evidence would suggest that where these are inadequately followed up, gains are eventually wiped out. The remedial teaching of spelling did form part of Collins's research (1961). The main teaching methods were those of Schonell, using diagnostic prescriptive teaching based on patterns of error, analysed in terms of visual and auditory discrimination. Collins found that such categorization of errors was unhelpful and that Schonell's drills had little effect:

> An analysis of the spelling test papers of the research sample proved that one and the same child makes all types of errors and these errors are not corrected by remedial drills.

Collins supposed that while perception plays an important part in the learning of spelling, there are other rather more important conceptual processes involved. This corresponds with recent findings in cognitive psychology (e.g. Frith: 1980, Bransford: 1979). Gates and Schonell conceived of visual and auditory perception as functions of the brain seated in diverse and discrete areas. Findings from more recent neurological investigations suggest that given visual stimuli affect large areas of the brain. Whilst we might think we can 'see' the Acropolis or our house in our mind's eye, the analogy of a photographic record breaks down on closer analysis:

> Propositions can be used to represent knowledge that is assumed to be abstract and conceptual, rather than linguistic, visual, tactile. For example, many computer programs can create dynamic visual displays, but the basis of these displays is propositional. Our ability to generate images of our home or our car need not therefore imply that we actually store images. By the same token

our ability to produce words and sentences need not imply that we store actual words and sentences.
(Bransford: 1979: p. 191)

We may think we can see the spelling of a word or hear whether it 'sounds' right, yet it may not be that visual or aural image which underlies our knowledge of spelling. A more fruitful analogy might be to cognitive data. As we learn more about reading and language, we increase our store of generalizations about words, word shapes and word functions. This has been referred to by cognitive psychologists as the lexical data base. It is constructed according to our view of the rules of language which need not necessarily correspond with formal spelling or grammatical rule systems. We simply make sense of the structures as best we can. English spelling has three functions. Firstly it offers a complex and not entirely consistent medium for the translation of sounds and visual symbols. The eccentricities of this medium can easily be demonstrated by reference to the poem sent anonymously to 'The Sunday Times' (3.1.65) of which this is the last verse:

A moth is not a moth in mother
Nor both in bother, broth in brother,
And here is not a match for there,
Nor dear and fear and bear and pear,
And then there's dose and rose and lose -
Just look them up - and goose and choose,
And cork and work and card and ward,
And font and front and word and sword,
And do and go and thwart and cart -
Come, come, I've hardly made a start!
A dreadful language? Man alive.
I'd mastered it when I was five.

Part of the reason for such diversity is that the second function of spelling is that it contains information about the history and etymology of words. It also offers syntactical cues to the reader. Whilst these would be redundant in a strictly logical spelling code, the fact that the sound 'et' could be spelt ate, et, ette or ebt offers the reader different cues about its own meaning and those of the surrounding words.

Poor spelling may arise from direct sensory handicap - like an untreated sight loss or intermittent catarrhal deafness. It might also develop because the child has a faulty or incomplete grasp of the probabilities of letter-sound combinations, which would also undermine his intuitive understanding of the historical and etymological cues. Or it might be because the child makes insufficient use of what has been referred to as a lexical 'buffer' (Morton: 1977). He fails to check his spelling either word by word or by proof reading afterwards. A certain amount of poor spelling is institutionalized. A backward reader may only have attained a limited sight vocabulary and phonic store by the time he leaves the infant school. His sense of left-right orientation is unlikely to be as well established as that of a better reader. He might find it more difficult to co-ordinate the visual order of the symbols with the temporal order of the sounds. In junior school, however, his class teacher may well expect him to be able to practice his reading on his own and spend far more time writing. Whilst this may well develop the reading and spelling skills of the average and advanced pupils by encouraging them to guess at unfamiliar words and relating phonic data to meaning directly, such psycholinguistic guessing games (Goodman: 1970) might disrupt the backward speller's poorly developed lexical store. He will need to be taught much more about words which high expectation pupils pick up quite unselfconsciously as they read (Peters: 1967).

By the end of junior school the forward readers will be able to analyse long words into syllables, holding sound and morphemic units in mind, whilst spelling their way through the word. Without consciously doing so, they refer to their lexical 'buffer', checking that the sequence of letters looks right and the strokes of the pen feel right (Hotopf: 1980). By now they will have most of the letter sound permutations and be able to predict in a rough and ready way the likelihood of using certain combinations in certain words. Given nonsense syllables they will be able to spell them in a predictable way (Frith: 1980). As they reach the secondary school, they will also learn which words they are uncertain of and how to use a dictionary to correct themselves. Without sympathetic help, the otherwise able child with poor spelling might have started to mistrust his 'buffer'. Given nonsense syllables to spell, he seems to lack the background of associated data and he may continue to make omissions and reversals. Both he and the low expectation pupil may well have resorted to poor handwriting as a screen for their spelling errors. So much of the basic vocabulary of English is irregularly spelt that the poor reader might not have grasped many of the less common letter sound serial patterns. So insecure is he that he might stick to patterns he knows rather than update them with more sophisticated exceptions.

Yet the emphasis in so many secondary schools is on speed of writing. Bad habits are reinforced where for poor spellers the aim should be to revise and refurbish parts of the lexical store. It may well be that the best way to do this is for subject teachers to emphasize spelling patterns across the curriculum (Peters: 1967). Spelling could thus be seen as one aspect of a complex pattern of linguistic development which would include the development of oral and reading vocabularies, knowledge of letter sound combinations and morphemes and the desire to communicate through writing. Such a desire would have an interactional component. The pupil would need to feel that the teacher was encouraging him to take risks and willing to help and explain spelling patterns before he could be persuaded to update his own model of the spelling rules.

Under pressure to correct spelling errors, the teacher may use a programmed learning kit like the Basil Blackwell Spelling Workshop (1975). This is one of the most successful the author has used and it appears to have a positive effect on children throughout the range of spelling ability. Yet the reliability with individual children who have pronounced spelling difficulties is not high. Just as successful are lessons in the history of language. With each linguistic input one could explain some of the main sources of error in a given class. If one were talking about Anglo-Saxon, one could clarify the 'doubling' rule. Children with a poorly developed lexical 'buffer' often find difficulty knowing when to double consonants and when not. Neither variant 'looks' right and the only way to sort out confusions at this intuitive level is to present correct examples, get the class to induce the rules and exceptions, then internalize them through examples. As the history of language moves forward to the Renaissance, one can explain much about suffixes, prefixes and morphemes. Children at all levels of spelling ability can be encouraged to make word families using this kind of building block approach, inventing new words and defining them for fun. Herbert Kohl (1967) describes how lessons about the derivation of Greek words and the Greek alphabet provided the foundation of his relationship with the thirty six alienated and low achieving children from Harlem:

> One day Ralph cursed at Michael and unexpectedly things came together for me. Michael was reading and stumbled several times. Ralph scornfully called out "What's the matter, psyches, going to pieces again?" The class broke up and I jumped on the word "psyches".
>
> "Ralph, what does psyches mean?"
>
> An embarrassed silence.
>
> "Do you know how to spell it?"
>
> Alvin volunteered "s-i-k-e-s"
>
> "Where do you think the word came from? Why did everybody laugh when you said it, Ralph?"
>
> "You know, Mr. Kohl, it means like crazy or something."
>
> "Why? How do words mean what they do?"

Suggesting that spelling does have a meaning and allowing children to express their fascination with language may well start them wanting to write, which itself breaks through self-fulfilling prophecies about illiteracy. When the author compared a group who had spent half a term using programmed approaches with another which had spent the same time on a history of spelling, both classes made marginally more than a year's progress. In both cases, however, only half the poor readers and children with marked discrepancies between general ability and spelling performance made this kind of progress and some made none at all. However, children who failed to make progress for long periods may suddenly catch up later. It may be more effective to have a systematic policy for the teaching of spelling so that all children are exposed to programmed kits and histories of spelling at different times in their careers rather than remedial tuition on a once and for all basis. Some schools have a spelling policy arranged by the Head of the English Department as part of a language policy across the curriculum and also run voluntary spelling clubs where poor spellers can go for individual attention, whatever their general level of ability. The spelling club would then be organised by the Co-ordinator for Special Educational Needs or the Head of English.

Whilst short term intensive courses may prove helpful to some children with 'blocks' about handwriting and grammar, there is little to suggest that it would provide reliable long term gains for large numbers of children. Some grammatical 'errors' represent sub-cultural patterns which are as logical in their own contexts as the rules of standard English (Labov: 1969). The process of reflecting and legitimating these patterns whilst conveying that they only represent part of the repertoire is a lengthy and ambiguous one. Many low expectation pupils find the notion of sentences difficult to grasp and merely penalizing their work for a lack of full stops and capital letters may discourage writing. As they tell a story orally they link the units of meaning with an 'and' and use the rhythm of the narrative to provide pauses. When asked to write a story or an essay, they expect to be able to achieve the same effect. If they have a reading ago of 8.5 or less some of their books might segment prose by putting phrases on different lines, thus using the beginning and ends of phrases and the climaxes of the story as markers. They have less exposure to the full stop rules. The concept of audience is a way out of this dilemma. Where pupils are going to show their work to each other, parents or employers, they will appreciate the need for flexibility. As a rule of thumb they can be told that in formal exercises they should use no more than two 'and's' in a sentence and that no sentence should be more than two lines long. At the end of a writing lesson they can be asked to proof read work that is going to be displayed, applying the 'two rules'. Fitting this kind of approach into remedial or special class curricula or just limiting it to pupils for whom there are the most limited expectations, seems short sighted. The pupils might only proof read in this special environment. In other classes where they are pressed to produce long stretches of writing which may not be marked very carefully for grammatical and spelling errors by subject specialists, they may not generalize what they have learned. It might be more effective for the learning Consultant to play a larger part in a language policy group, helping subject specialists to improve children's language performance in their own areas rather than merely withdrawing children on a voluntary basis.

The Co-ordination of Special Education

Galletley (op cit: 1975) thought that the main aim of these voluntary remedial groups should be to convince other staff that they could do the job as well as he could, thus bringing about the demise of his own department. Considering the chronic and intransigent nature of 'mild learning difficulties' in our educational system, this seems rather an optimistic aim. A more cautious approach would be to conceive of the Head of Remedial as a Co-ordinator of Special Education. The main aim of this role would be to ensure that low expectation pupils and pupils with particular difficulties were taught in stimulating and appropriate ways across the curriculum. Where this was not done, the co-ordinator would act as interceptor. There would be six major aspects of this role. The first would be to train a cross section of capable and sympathetic subject staff in the teaching of reading. The second would be to help set up or work with an English Across the Curriculum Group so as to extend staff understanding of the implications of differences in reading and writing ability. The third would be to develop the capabilities of low expectation pupils in mathematics. The fourth would be to enhance the capabilities of teachers in other subject departments with low expectation pupils. The fifth would be to develop more positive links between the community and those who are nearest to the borderline of what ordinary schools will tolerate - the slow, the troublesome, those with physical or sensory disabilities. In order to sustain that role, the sixth function would be to support the teachers who 'reach out forcefully and successfully to low achievers' (Brophy and Good: 1974). Most of these would already have worked with the co-ordinator in the teaching of reading. As an additional recognition of their value, they could also be given responsibility within their department for resources for special education. Elizabeth Jackson (1981) suggests that such a co-ordinator should be known as the Named Teacher; yet in a large comprehensive school it may be more helpful to conceive of each department having its own Named Teacher. These would continue to work with all levels of ability for some of the time, thus maintaining their own expectations, but would be expected to develop courses, materials and expertise with low expectation pupils particularly in mind. There might be a named teacher working in English, Social Studies, Science, Mathematics and Craft. Part of the time they would be teaching reading, part of the time teaching their subject speciality to average and able pupils and part of the time taking low stream or special classes. It might thus be possible to build up a group of like minded staff prepared to talk about common curricular problems but from the viewpoint of their own academic discipline, whilst simultaneously providing the subject departments with information and insight about the overcoming of low expectations. Not all the teachers of reading would work as named teachers. Many are just as forceful and successful with average and high expectation pupils and would no doubt have other responsibilities within the school. These might in fact make them as influential within their departments as the named teachers. The overall aim of this approach would be to extend areas of the school where pupils who deviate most from 'the middle of the road' (Sewell: 1981: op cit) can be relied upon to be given an appropriate and stimulating education.

Just as the teaching of reading formed the basis of 'remedial education' so the training of teachers in the teaching of reading is the starting point in this conception of co-ordinated special education. In the author's own experience, it did not take long to prepare most teachers. At the beginning of the academic year there were six lunch-hour in-service meetings. All staff were notified but those who were timetabled to teach reading were especially invited. The topics and lecture style might be chosen to reflect the particular interests of the teachers. One year there might be a lecture on 'dyslexia' so as to follow up a television programme. The notion of a discrepancy between reading ability and general intelligence can be discussed with a quick reference to the uncertain neurological and chemotherapeutic evidence about causes. Many teachers appear to be more interested in the methods which supporters of the notion, like Edith Norrie (1939), Grace Fernald (1943), Hornsby and Shear (1975), Cotterell (1969) and Professor Miles (1970) have developed in order to help intelligent children read and spell. This can itself be exploited so as to underline how inventive the teachers of reading may need to be in order to solve every individual child's difficulties.

With one course where the hardware happened to be available, the first lecture featured a video tape. The teacher was shown working on a one-to-one basis with one of the most troublesome pupils in the school, so as to demonstrate interaction. The skill of the teacher was in knowing how and when to intervene to generate the highest expectations in the pupil. Where children read sentences correctly there was tactful praise. Where children made a mistake, then realized what they had done, returned and corrected themselves, this was even more warmly received. Where the children made a mistake which undermined the sense of what they were reading, they might be allowed to read on until the end of the sentence, in the hope that the full context would alert them to the error. In the case of gross distortions of meaning, they might be stopped and asked to look at the word again. If that failed, they would be told what the word was. Where concentration seemed to lapse or panic set in, the child would be allowed to rest from the decoding process and invited instead to reflect on what he was reading. Questions about the meaning would be asked to cue the pupil into the context again, or a sentence might be read by the teacher.

The narrowness of the line between supporting children and encouraging them to take risks was emphasized. On this course, some of the teachers were critical of the video because at one point the reading teacher had asked the pupil a question about the passage and then, after the boy had replied "I don't know", had refused to tell him. It conflicted with their own image of the kindly remedial teacher, always willing to help or explain. The idea that it might help the poor reader to understand that he does not comprehend what he is reading seemed too much like a personal attack on his identity as a learner. Yet in the discussion it became clear that the audience accepted that there was good rapport between teacher and learner and that the boy himself did not appear to be threatened. The audience also knew from their classroom experience that many children quickly scan quite complex passages of prose without comprehending them or realizing that such an activity was pointless. However, it was also stressed that every teacher has his own ways of piquing curiosity and his own intuitions about how much pressure children could take. Confidence in one's own judgements as a teacher were of the first importance.

A third lecture might be about matching pupils and books. The teachers would be shown some of the norm referenced tests in use in the school, such as Burt, Schonell, Daniels and Diack (1958), GAP, etc. Whilst they all referred to the same concept - the child's reading age - they measured different aspects of reading. Burt and Schonell measure the ability to recognise and correctly pronounce certain words out of context. GAP reflects the ability to use contextual cues to guess simple words. Both skills are important in learning to read and while the word recognition test looks more concrete and reliable, research about reading tends to suggest that most readers spend most of their energies making guesses about words. The notion of a reading age was then examined critically. A child of five with a reading age of eight probably read in quite a different way from a child of eleven with a similar score, yet the test result itself told one little about differences in skills, attitudes and background understandings or about how these could be used to help the child. There might be little meaning in the difference between a score of 8.2 and 8.5. Few reading tests have been calibrated to reflect short term individual gains and those that are used tend to lose any reliability if practised on. Lastly the tests would be demonstrated either on film if this was available or by role play.

The second part of this third lecture would be about readability levels. The subject staff would be encouraged to bring along their own textbooks and worksheets and shown how to apply Fry's test (Fry: 1977). With teachers who had just begun to teach small groups of poor readers, this made them even more aware of the unsuitability of many materials. However, just because a child had a reading age of nine and the book's readability level was ten, it did not necessarily mean the book was unsuitable. The child might want to read it or he might be encouraged to read it in a suitable class context. On the other hand, just because a book seemed within the child's reading ability, it did not mean the child could be relied upon to read it on his own. Mathematics books in particular often use short sentences and familiar words yet their conceptual content is often conveyed extremely concisely. Without a teacher's help the prose 'surface' seems unbreakable to the child. For the special reading group itself it may be that a poorly motivated and careless reader may need to start the year with reading material that is well within his capacity. At the same time, if he had a special interest he might well be able to tackle books that are formally beyond him. The emphasis of recent research (e.g. Clay: 1977; Tansley and Panckhurst: 1981) has been to suggest that using the information from norm referenced tests as a guide, the teacher should develop her own expertise. In the author's reading department, each child had a record card with a graph on the front where formal scores could be plotted and a space on the back for more qualitative remarks. There was a colour coded reading library too and by matching the two, subject specialists had a sensible starting point for their year's work.

The fourth lecture might be about phonics. This has been the traditional mainstay of remedial education. Monroe was arguing in 1932 that unless phonic errors were analysed and corrected, they could persist for years. Tansley's Sound Sense (1975) and other books of word attack exercises have been used to the exclusion of all reading practice. Whilst it is important for teachers of reading to know the range and intricacy of English letter-sound combinations and to appreciate the value of regular and careful teaching of these schemes, a co-ordinated approach to special education would stress that the mistakes children make must be seen in the context of their reading strategies.

The chapter on The Reading Process in the Bullock Report (H.M.S.O.: 1975: pp. 77-96) contains some illuminating examples of phoneme grapheme correspondences. The letter 'o' has seven associated sounds, the sound 'I' twelve letter combinations, as follows:-

(i) one home comes women or of to
(ii) aisle height eye I phial ice high
island buy guide stye rhyme.

Gill Cotterell (1969) has published a check list of basic sounds, prefixes, endings, hard sounds and rules. This can be used in combination with audio tapes of children reading. It becomes obvious that only occasionally do these errors make simple kinds of pattern. The child might even get one phonic combination right six times and wrong the seventh. In discussion of these tapes, teachers might find a host of reasons for each mistake and treating every child as if he was ignorant of the correspondence could well be inappropriate. The child might have picked up miscues from the line above, suffered a lapse in concentration or made the wrong psycholinguistic guess. The precision teaching of phonics which could be demonstrated through the use of Alpha to Omega flash cards and dictation exercises, for example, (Hornsby and Shear: 1975) would still have a place in reading teaching, but it would be secondary to reading practice and sensitive teacher intervention. Hence as a conclusion to this fourth lecture, the co-ordinator would show the subject staff the way he makes his own informal notes of the reading characteristics of his group.

The fifth lecture might be about word recognition and attack skills. The Ladybird list of Key Words (Murray: 1969) is one of the most vivid illustrations of the phonic irregularity at the heart of our lexicon. Most secondary school children will have grasped the first 300 words anyway, but it is important that the minority who have not do so as quickly and as thoroughly as possible. Flashcards and games that may be played with them can be demonstrated.

Most adults know that fluency in reading unfamiliar words depends on syllabification. We have to 'chunk' such a word and syllables constitute a chunk of sound. All syllables have to contain at least one vowel and the commonest pattern is consonant-vowel-consonant. There are other patterns: vowel-consonant; consonant-vowel; vowel digraphs and consonant clusters. Yet if prefixes and suffixes can be learned separately, most long words split quite easily into three letter syllables. If this rule of thumb is used, reading teachers do not have to insist their pupils learn to tell the difference between vowels and consonants or the range of syllabic forms. It may be that some of the long words which children learn to syllabify out of context never form part of their thinking vocabulary anyway, so they might not use them again or remember how they should be pronounced.

Another way of 'chunking' long and unfamiliar words is by reference to 'morphemes'. When we read we recognise that certain parts of the word are familiar and that they have a meaning similar to parts of other long words. The morpheme 'graph' is common to telegraph, graphic, etc., 'vision' to television, revision and so on.

The final part of the fifth lecture could be about how to use 'family trees' of words as a way of building up other linguistic contexts as an aid to word recognition and vocabulary extension. Terms like prefixes, suffixes and morphemes need never be employed, but the use of linguistic patterns in order to guess at meanings and pronounciations can be encouraged.

The sixth lecture might be about comprehension. The concept of SQ3R might be outlined in terms of the SRA reading laboratory (Parker: 1963). The children are encouraged to look through the whole exercise, including the picture, the subheadings in the story and the questions as a way of cuing in their reading. Many seem to enjoy the structure and learn something from the apparatus for half a term or so, providing they are put on the scheme at an appropriate level and not allowed to cheat their way onto higher cards. A parody of the programmed approach to comprehension can be shown, demonstrating the way background knowledge and a feeling for syntactical cues can be used to provide answers to nonsensical questions:

> Having culpted the Akzendrites in the merches of Xeph, Piat faped a mathik. He smocked the Akzendrite parits, ster the Akzendrite Macrodon and appronted fittily. So ritulous was his acsimony that he exoriated the Dendrious and tortilated the Macrious. The Oriopticites, a nerquid paramit, were also mignopulated.
>
> Questions:
>
> 1. Where did the Piat attack the Akzendrites?
>
>   A In the merches of Xeph
>   B In the mathik
>   C Near the parits.
>
> 2. What was the leader of the Akzendrites called?
>
>   A Dendrious
>   B Fittily
>   C The Macrodon.
>
> 3. Which tribes were beaten by Piat's army?

As an alternative to the programmed approach to comprehension, the teachers could be shown how to build reflective reading into children's practice. As well as telling the teacher what had just happened or what a certain character had just done, the pupils could be encouraged to guess what would happen next or what the next page might be about. The dreariness of mechanically reading round a circle to improve accuracy or fluency without ever stopping to talk about the story could be stressed. One of the attributes of the stereotypical slow learner is that he loses concentration all too easily. We have seen how this may impede literal reading skills already. Yet there is a time and a place for having a think about the book, switching the words off and letting one's imagination come to the fore. Like talking in class, dreaming is often made to seem wrong. Yet privacy plays a vital role in the interpretative aspects of reading and these are necessary for the accretion of extended contextual schema. Modern structuralist approaches to reading stress the fact that we can never know what another person makes of a given text. Imaginative prose is so full of ambiguity that by asking questions of it, we almost certainly impose certain meanings on it and shut out certain others.

This would suggest that although comprehension follows decoding skills at an historical level, the two proceed very much in tandem, especially for older pupils with incomplete decoding skills. Some phonic or word recognition errors follow quite logically from a misunderstanding. Goodman (1970) argues that when reading, mature readers catch the drift of a passage then interpret the words on the page to fit their hypotheses. Occasionally they know that what they thought was on the pages did not make sense so they check it, reading certain sections more carefully word for word. For the older backward reader however, years of miscues and misunderstandings may have conveyed the message that school books are full of nonsense anyway. Hence there is little point in reflecting on what one has read in the light of one's own experience. Comprehension exercises, so popular because they seem to render the reading process assessable, might further distract the pupil from an understanding of a passage in his own terms.

For the teacher, the decision whether to emphasize decoding skills or meaning in any given context is part of his professional judgement. The practicalities can be illustrated through video or lesson transcript like the following:

> The period between the end of the First World War and .. in 1819 .. 1918 and a beginning of the Second World War was one which was considerably (teacher: what's the first letter?) saw considerable (teacher: very good) experiments on airships .. some men throughout that (teacher: some men ..) thought that the airships ..

This fifteen year old, Michael, is making numbers of reversal errors and is guessing at familiar irregular words. In the first instance the teacher allows the pupil to correct '1819' from his store of knowledge. In the second, reversing 'saw' led to another error 'considerably' and a considerable lexical distortion, so the teacher hastened to remind Michael of its initial letter. In the third instance the teacher emphasises the syntactical context. Michael had had years of phonic exercises and despaired of ever learning to read. There were periods when all sense went out of his reading. With such children it is often necessary to rest from decoding, talk about the book, the topic, the child's experience of school, so as to reinforce the idea that education is significant, what the pupil does in school has meaning and that a book represents the possibility of a medium between himself and significant knowledge.

At the conclusion of this sixth lecture, staff can be shown how to make dictated experience books for very poor and very alienated readers (Stauffer: 1970). Where published materials have failed, the child may be encouraged to talk about himself to the point where he tells the teacher stories of his life. The teacher tapes these or copies them down, edits a few of the most difficult words or sentences, yet preserving the rhythms and idioms of the child's own speech. Illustrations can be added and the whole book presented as the child's own reader. One such book was prepared for Keith, a boy who had been previously ascertained as ESN, maladjusted, partially sighted and dyslexic. He had been sent to an ESN(M) school and transferred to the Remedial Department of an ordinary school. Despite all the drills he had been taught, Keith had only learned to recognise three words on the Schonell Test. Within a few weeks of working on this kind of autobiographical material, he had learned fifteen or twenty of the test words. Such stories often have a definite aesthetic and moral shape. They reflect the children's dialect and individual speech styles. In this instance the illustrations were made by an art teacher at the school. They were deliberately contrived to appear like those of a comic. The whole experience provides an apt example of this co-ordinated concept of special education. Comprehension preceded and made possible the development of primary skills. If the text had held no meaning for Keith, he would not have learned the words that made it up. By communicating his sense of meaning to the reading teacher, he was helping to teach the staff how to teach him. This called on the talents of staff whose main subject was not 'special education' and whose main responsibility was 'middle of the road' children. In so doing, it defeated the extraordinarily low expectations which a full psychological assessment had formalized.

In one lecture the subject staff would probably want some guidance about how to arrange lessons and a curriculum. Even in a group of five or six, the needs of the children might be quite at variance with one another. One might have a reading age of nine, yet be so careless that he understands little of what he reads. One might be slow and accurate, yet just responding to print mechanically without comprehension. A third might not have finished his learning of the alphabet and have a sight vocabulary of 100 words. The notion of different forms of grouping and individualized learning would then have to be discussed in sensible and practical terms.

As these formal reading teaching sessions came to an end there was often a considerable feeling on unease. Whilst staff said they had found these working lunches enjoyable and interesting, they felt little better at coping with the real task of teaching children to read. It was not easy to reassure them that experience was the best teacher and that they would each adapt these ideas to suit themselves. In these circumstances, staff groups have asked the author to give an extra demonstration session. The backward readers with the most robust personalities are asked if they would mind showing other teachers what a reading lesson is like. It is emphasized that these teachers will be concentrating on the co-ordinator, not the children. The actual demonstration is kept short and the children rewarded for their trouble. The staff are invited to ask their questions when the children have left.

Despite this practical guidance, there is still a great amount of uncertainty. It is here that one begins to appreciate the human costs of a co-ordinated approach to low expectation pupils. Staff are being asked to move across subject boundaries and deal with group sizes that are unfamiliar. There is often a sense of despair about ever getting the group they are responsible for to learn anything. This seems to mask a deeper disquiet about the children in their subject lessons whose general understanding and reading had been just as poor. These children had taken part in the lessons, they even seemed to find them interesting, yet with so many other children in the room, there had never been time for the teacher to get to know how much they really understood.

Painful though this period can be, it can have its positive aspects. It can lead to a more general renewal of interest in curricula and school organization. The author assumed that once started, this process would lead to a gradual evolutionary change in staff attitudes and teaching strategies. Whilst it is true that some departments adapted their work quite considerably after the involvement of one of their members in reading teaching, others continued to 'pigeon hole' remedial work. They did not seem to realize that low status pupils needed similar support in subject lessons. Hence the second major responsibility of the Co-ordinator of Special Education could be defined as developing the staff's sensitivity about the linguistic demands made in subject lessons on low expectation pupils.

The first aspect of this role is the revision and extension of subject libraries and worksheets. The second is to ensure that all departments realize the difficulties many pupils, not merely the low expectation pupils, have skimming, scanning and organizing lengthy pieces of text, especially where these contain large amounts of subject jargon. The third is to co-ordinate a school approach to spelling. The fourth is to ensure that experiments in teaching methods which seem to have special relevance to those with language and reading difficulties are tried out.

Where Language Across the Curriculum Committees exist and seem to be effective, the co-ordinator can work through these. Copies of readability formulae like Fry's (1977) can be brought to meetings and applied to texts in common use. Teachers of Science or History can be shown examples of the Nottingham Reading for Learning Project (to be published). There are workshop exercises which teachers can use to develop their own understanding of text organization. Lunzer and Gardner (1977; and to be published) show how in Science or Craft lessons, part of the reading is often a list of instructions. Pupils may not find out what to do by reading them, however, or they may read them without understanding. In order to heighten their awareness of the reading process, the list is cut into sentences which are then jumbled. The pupils have to work out which order makes sense. This may lead some of the class to formulate hypotheses before a scientific experiment is carried out and use the experiment to verify the theory, as is prescribed by the scientific method.

Reading lessons in English either mean that the whole class is reading the same book, so effectively excluding 'remedial children' or that different groups are given different books, so reinforcing pupil expectations. If the first method was adopted, class discussions seemed to involve only average and able children. Here again, low expectation children found themselves excluded even though their needs to join in a discussion were as great, if not greater, than anyone else's. The loan of a video camera from an F.E. college made it possible for members of the Language Across the Curriculum Group from the author's school to look at their own teaching styles and to develop new ones. Brophy and Good (1974) found this form of micro teaching was one of the few reliable methods for helping teachers 'learn sophisticated and comprehensive strategies for dealing with academic failures'. In so many cases, teachers asked closed questions. They used questions as a disciplinary tool, controlling the attention of low ability and alienated pupils. They did not wait long for low expectation pupils to answer and when they did they often repeated the answer, thus making the child's contribution redundant.

We found, though, that where a class could be relied upon to be quiet and attentive and direct their remarks to the class through the teacher, it was possible to develop teaching strategies that would undermine these expectations. The teacher tells the class that from that moment on, he is not going to ask them any more questions. The rules of the discussion lesson have changed. He will pause from time to time during the reading of a poem, for instance, and allow the class to ask him questions instead. At first we found that most children were uncertain. They do not know what the teacher wants from them and they suspect his motives. They then start to ask questions they think he wants to hear. At last a child plucks up sufficient courage to ask the teacher a question he thinks will catch him out. The class realizes that something unusual is about to happen and, when the teacher does not try to evade these difficult questions, more join in. The class now taste something of the academic pursuit. They scent out their expert's weaknesses and eventually a question is asked which the teacher can not answer. He may be able to find it in the quiet of a library and he may think of it ten minutes after leaving the classroom, but in the tension of that lesson he does not know. The way in which he handles this problem is of crucial importance. If he admits he does not know, that the class has indeed caught him out, the school failures may realize that the teacher is in some respects just like them. If the teacher explains that in educational terms, it is to be *hoped* that experts will be found wanting, children who have never wanted to play a part in discussions because they cannot win, will also join in.

Fairly soon after this discovery the class begins to realize there are trick questions which are only designed to help the questioner show off and good questions which merit an answer. It may take two weeks' lessons to arrive at this point but the teacher says he is going to change the rules of the discussion lesson once again. From now on not only will he refuse to ask questions, he will refuse to answer them as well.

He will merely act the role of a chairperson asking for questions, then passing back to the class to answer them. His role is still mainly to keep good order, but he is not going to shape the discussion in any way. He will ensure that everyone who wants to can get a good hearing.

The last stage in the evolution of this form of mixed ability teaching is to wait until the class can operate these new rules then seize on a question to which the pupil appears to want to know the answer. The question is a good question in the sense that the pupil did not know the answer before he asked it, he is not trying to catch anyone, he is simply curious. In terms of pacing his response, the teacher gives the pupil sufficient time to reflect then asks the pupil 'What do you think?' The child's first response will often be 'That's not fair! I did not expect to have to answer my own question.' The teacher persists, even though the child looks lost and anxious. Instead of competing with the rest of the class, he is competing with himself. He does not run any risk of being shown up for if he does not know, the teacher lets the question go. It is that child's question and no-one else will be allowed to answer it for him. Perhaps ten days later he will come up with an answer. Most children however find that they can answer such questions and when their anxiety dies down they realize that this allows them to think in school in ways they never suspected they could have done.

In one lesson where this technique was in use, we were discussing the point in Coleridge's 'Ancient Mariner' where the dead men rise:

> They groaned, they stirred, they all uprose,
> Nor spoke, nor moved their eyes.
> It had been strange, even in a dream,
> To have seen those dead men rise.

The mixed ability class of thirteen year olds had been subjecting the poem to textual analysis in their own terms over several days and we had reached the point familiar to most scholars where we could no longer see the wood for the trees. An able and original boy asked the quite genuine question 'What does this poem mean?' At that point no-one knew, the teacher no more than the pupils. There was a pause in which the class contemplated their own limitations. At this point the pupil with the lowest IQ score and reading age answered: 'This poem's about beauty.' He referred us back to the stanzas in the previous part where the sea snakes had changed:

> ...   and every track
> Was a flash of golden fire.
>
> O Happy living things! no tongue
> Their beauty might declare
> A spring of love gush'd from my heart
> And I bless'd them unawares.

Even in the most competitive, selective class of thirteen year olds, the ability to link what appeared to be an image of resurrection and these earlier references to blessing and beauty would have been beyond the most confident high expectation pupils. Because the element of risk was lower and everyone felt safe to contribute, a boy who had every reason to scorn English lessons, poetry appreciation especially, had done so. Having conceived of that larger pattern, the rest of the class could elaborate on it. Having made the remark, the low expectation pupil felt no need to show off. He was only one of twenty five who spoke in that lesson. His contribution, although exceedingly sharp, was merely apt in such a context.

Other colleagues were invited to watch the group and play the new role. A video film was made and the results were shown to a wider audience in the staff. Although the technique was especially suited to a subject like English where the meaning of the lesson content was always ambiguous, it was also tried in Sociology and Environmental Studies. In lexical and micro-sociological terms it has much in common with the small group discussions outlined by Dolan, Dolan, Taylor, Shoreland and Harrison in Chapter Nine of The Effective Use of Reading (Lunzer and Gardner: 1977). Mixed ability groups set to work on textual analysis, asking questions of each other in their own language and in their own terms. The classic justifications of English method are often made in relation to an individualized approach to practical criticism, epitomized in the university teaching of I.A. Richards (1929) and implying a hierarchy of taste and intelligence. Yet in these approaches any such hierarchy becomes the subject of public dispute. The authority of all the individuals in the class is in competition with each others' <u>and</u> that of the teacher. In such circumstances, pupils seen as 'stupid' or 'delinquescent' (Hargreaves: op cit 1968) are able to play a more prominent and constructive role in the lesson. Conversely, the convergent thinkers who normally succeed in guessing what the teacher wanted them to say were now extremely angry.

Allowing pupils to ask and answer questions which are real for them has implications in the politics of knowledge. As the Nottingham Reading for Learning Project team also found, it appears to throw the assumed 'range of ability' into question. Pupils whose identity as educational successes depended on their providing convergent answers to closed questions had to learn a new set of rules about what constituted 'thinking'. This was no doubt a painful process yet, as Jules Henry has pointed out, the alternative has its own perils. 'Giving teacher what she wants' (1955) breeds docility and undermines independence of thought amongst middle class high achievers, just as the downward negotiations of low achievers reinforce their alienation.

Teachers of English seem to be more successful with low expectation pupils despite the preponderance of reading and writing in their lessons (e.g. Brennan: 1979). In a report on research conducted in this area, Partington and Hinchliffe

(1979) argue that the way English teachers conduct discussions has a great deal to do with this. They argued that the style of leadership was more often 'integrative' than 'dominant' and that this allows for greater class involvement. Teacher-pupil exchanges were longer, more sophisticated and elaborate and English teachers seemed to respond to pupils at a more personal level. Their implication was that identification of a pupil's difficulties was much less significant than identification with those difficulties.

The problems that teachers of mathematics have with low expectation children have been much more amply documented at both a personal and professional level (e.g. Abelwhite: 1969: Low Attainers in Mathematics Schools Council Project: to be published). Brennan (1979) argues that mathematics teachers often fail to identify the linguistic and conceptual schemes these pupils bring to the lessons. Classroom discussion breaks down because questions and explanations presuppose a mastery of formal thinking the children do not possess. This frustrates the children. Liam Hudson's analysis (1966) of the compartmentalization of emotion and intellect that procedes in many of the convergent thinking adolescents who later become mathematics graduates may help to explain why so many mathematics teachers base their authority on their knowledge of the subject rather than on an understanding of both the subject and the children.

Teachers who find no place in the learning process for inexactitude, emotion and intuition are unlikely to take a sympathetic interest in how children fail. Forced to accept that all pupils need to follow mathematics throughout their school lives, such staff might be happy to accede that a certain proportion of the year have special educational needs in their subject and should be taught in the Remedial Department or Resource Room. Historically speaking, teaching mathematics to slow learners has always had an important role in Remedial Education and special class teaching. It is assumed that because the reading teacher is 'good with backward children' and backwardness can be attributed across the basic subjects, she ought also to teach the low attainers in mathematics. Conceptually speaking, terms like 'remedial maths' and 'special mathematical needs' have little meaning, and the third major function of the Special Education Co-ordinator is to develop a critique of the mutual alienation of mathematics teachers and low attaining pupils and find practicable alternatives within the school.

Unlike reading, there are no commonly agreed criteria of competence in mathematics below which a child can be defined as backward, retarded or having special educational needs. This makes grounds for selection depend on the individual school's policies. Many simply give a mathematics examination to the whole year group and draw off a small group of children with the lowest scores. Although used in effect as a screening test, such an examination lacks norm referencing and takes little account of variations in mathematics curricula. Often they are so lacking in detail that it is often impossible to form a realistic view of which children have which kinds of problem in which area. Even if it were possible to generate norm referenced testing in 'mathematical concepts' successful 'remediation' would make nonsense of streaming arrangements since the first group would then be replaced as the bottom set by the group of children who originally had better scores. The strongest argument against terms like 'remedial maths' and 'special needs in maths' is that there is no mystique about the techniques used by effective teachers of bottom streams. Successful mathematics teachers at every level use words their children can understand, gauge pupil preparedness for new concepts, make detailed assessments, teach incrementally and diagnose the causes of inappropriate thinking. Most attempts to isolate the specifically 'remedial' or 'special' attributes of such groups do so in terms of curricular limitations and with little considerations this may have in terms of teacher-pupil expectations. Brennan (1979) for instance opens his discussion of mathematics in these terms:

> In this basic subject, with curricula mainly confined to essential skills and concepts, Table 5 indicates that successful curricula were observed in only one in four primary, one in six secondary and one in eight special schools.

Remedial Mathematics groups may have developed because they suited the professional claims of both mathematics and remedial staff. Excluding the least able from mainstream teaching has the advantage of giving the mathematics department a degree of exclusivity. Unfortunately non-specialist mathematics staff often lack confidence in their own understanding of the subject. Many remedial or special class teachers often have a background in junior school training or a degree in the Humanities. Some of the 'new Maths' which could supposedly help them to give the children more practical experience is beyond them. Hence their approach may be unnecessarily conservative and dogmatic. As Brennan and others have found, mathematics lessons frequently comprise pages of examples. Operations have to be carried out in such a way that the teacher himself feels safe, rather than that which corresponds most closely to the pupils' own conceptions.

Children develop their own ways of calculating and these often appear to wander far beyond the standard written algorithms prescribed by the teacher. John Holt (1964) gives an example of a girl called Betty, considered by some of her mathematics teachers as a slow pupil but who, in Holt's experience, 'liked to look at things from several angles to consider the meaning or meanings of what she is doing'.

> Betty said, 2/4 + 3/5 is 1 or more, you need two more fifths to make 1 and 2/4 is more than 2/5, so the answer must be bigger than 1.

Stuart Plunckett (1977) gives further examples with children, students and adults:

Me: Do you know what 7 lots of 8 are?
Peter (aged 7): No.
Me: Could you work it out?
Peter: (long pause) 56.
Me: How did you do that?
Peter: Well .. I know 10 8's, so I took away 8, that's 72, and another and another - 56.
Me: What's 213 take away 188?
Ray (adult): 25.
Me: How d'you do it?
Ray: Well it's 12 up to 200 and 13's 25.
Me: What's 213 take away 188?
Student (aged 19): Silence!
Me: What happened when I asked?
Student: Panic.
Me: Did you see anything in your mind ...
Student: Yes, I saw 213 written down and then 188 underneath it, and then a line ...

Teachers with an understanding of the four algebraic 'rules' which underpin our number system would appreciate that there is an infinitely large number of ways of approaching any particular calculation. The written algorithms often represent the most concise ways of tabulating them but where pupils who expect to fail are concerned, these formal methods may become less efficient than the longer rule of thumb strategies children concoct for themselves. This probably explains how the children in Herndon's 'Dumb Class' (referred to on page 47 above) could score bowling in the bowling alley but not in the classroom. Given the problem of penning groups of children in a restricted curriculum which they first covered at the age of seven and which they are obliged to repeat until they leave school, it may be more effective to let the children experiment with the algebraic properties of number than to give them fresh examples of the standard algorithms. This would undermine the special and remedial curricula 'mainly confined to essential skills and concepts' (Brennan) and it is unlikely to occur in an education system where teachers with a good understanding of the subject are wary of the slow learners and teachers who are 'good with the children' are wary of the subject.

As a way out of this impasse the Special Education Co-ordinator must first learn more of the discipline himself so that he knows something of the teaching skills required to teach low expectation pupils some algebra and geometry. Having demonstrated to his own satisfaction that this can in fact strengthen their grasp of survival skills, he can begin to communicate with specialist mathematics staff on their own ground. In-service courses for non-mathematics specialists may constitute a short cut, but not all Mathematics Education lecturers have a sympathetic understanding of the teachers' conceptual frameworks. It may be less confusing for the co-ordinator to take the pupils' CSE and 'O' level textbooks and work his way through them.

Having moved some of the way to the mathematics teachers' ground, the second stage is to invite their co-operation in devising diagnostic testing and profiling for the least able. Theoretically speaking, there is a limitless number of errors that can be made in any calculation, but with his experience of remedial mathematics groups, the special education co-ordinator will be able to outline a few of the main types which he and the mathematics staff can draw up tests for. Whilst it is by no means certain that specific errors can be accounted for by lack of knowledge of a certain operation, it may be useful to sample the same kind of operation over time and in different contexts. Whilst both correct answers and errors can mask variations in degrees of mastery, the results of these tests can be used to manufacture individual, class and year profiles which point out approximate areas of need and provide a yard-stick for further programme evaluation. Tests like these already exist, the Richmond series (Hieronymus et al: 1975) for instance. Yet the essential advantage of home produced materials is that it reinforces the identification of mathematics staff <u>with</u> low attaining pupils, as well as contributing to the identification of their needs. The overall aim of a co-ordinated approach to the teaching of mathematics to low expectation pupils is to enhance the teacher's understanding of how the children think.

Having brought about some co-operation on assessment, the third stage might be for the co-ordinator to help set up workshops on teaching itself. One might start with the problem of how to teach an algebraic understanding of the difference between squared numbers to a bottom stream class which contains unruly, alienated children and one or two children with moderate learning difficulties about whom statements are maintained. With this objective in mind, the teacher can end each of his ordinary lessons with a problem. This is a special problem in series, and the first correct answer may win a token. As the days progress the problems get more difficult, involving a wider range of calculations in whole numbers until at last the series of squared numbers is given:

1 ... 3 ... 5 ... 7 ... 9 ...
1 ... 3 ... 9 ... 27 ...
1 ... 4 ... 20 ... 23 ... 115 ... 118 ...
1 ... 4 ... 9 ... 16 ... 25 ... 36 ...

In other words, it will be expected that pupils will have to use their own algorithms and think inductively. This will involve them in a degree of risk taking. Whereas most risks involve failure, this is only a game. The pupil himself is his own best judge of whether the solution is correct. The right answer has a certain aesthetic appeal which he can then put into words to the rest of the class. If anyone fails to understand they are encouraged to ask the pupil why he thinks his answer is right. In the example of the differences between the squares, most low expectation pupils solve the problem as if it were a subtraction rather than a square. The difference between (1 ... 4) is 3, (4 ... 9) is 5, (9 ... 16) is 7, (16 ... 25) is 9, (25 ... 36) is 11, so the next in the series must be 36 add 13 is 49. In the next lesson all reference to that problem can be dropped and the group asked to make number patterns with squares:

The squares can be cumulative rather than separate and the children asked to guess how many more pegs they will need to make the next square. By trial and error the children will work out that they need 7 for a 4 square, 9 for a 5 square, 11 for a 6 square and so on. When asked why, the children will no doubt say you need two sides and a corner. From this geometrical solution to the same problem the group can be referred back to the original arithmetical series. They now perceive that the problem referred to subtraction and squares and that there is a relationship between the number squared and the difference between the squared number and the next squared number. Teachers solving the problem in a workshop situation <u>and</u> low expectation pupils often express it in the same terms: 'It's two of the first number plus one'. You then ask them if this will always be so, whatever the first number is and they will realize that the previous geometrical example somehow proves it will be. Some time afterwards the group can be set the problem 100 x 100 take away 99 x 99. Some will no doubt try the standard written algorithm and succeed, lengthy though that process will be. Others who have begun to grasp what mathematics is about will start to look for a short cut. A few hints from the teacher about squared numbers, sides and corners will set some of these solving it in terms of either

$$2x + 1 : (2 \times 99) + 1 \quad \text{or} \quad (2y - 1) : (2 \times 100) - 1$$

These children might now be ready to substitute letters for numbers, however esoteric that may seem, because they are beginning to grasp that this is a universal rule and that particular numbers are in a sense irrelevant. Some time later after consolidating the notion that you can perform certain mathematical operations with any number, the children can be asked to convert $99^2 - 100^2$ into an algebraic formulation, then demonstrate by algebraic means that the difference between squared numbers is the two sides plus a corner:

$$\begin{aligned} & (a + 1)^2 - a^2 \\ = \; & (a + 1) \times (a + 1) - a^2 \\ = \; & a^2 + a + a + 1 - a^2 \\ = \; & 2a + 1 \end{aligned}$$

Taking low expectation groups through intellectual operations of this degree of abstraction demands weeks of careful planning, a readiness to reinforce half formed concepts in words children understand and a strong relationship. These are the same characteristics of effective special education in terms of reading, History and Geography as we have previously defined it. It differs so minutely from the characteristics of good teaching generally that it could be carried out in any mathematical setting, whether called a special class, remedial mathematics or a mixed ability group, if only the teacher is capable of fertility of mind and the personal commitment. In the experience of the author, workshop accounts of successful experiments in the teaching of geometry and algebra are swamped by suggestions from mathematics staff. Their familiarity with the higher reaches of the subject will allow them to bring forward a much wider range of problems which the low expectation pupil can be encouraged to tackle. This process of reconsidering apparently immutable hierarchies of knowledge from the perspective of such children, can kindle a deeper interest in the children themselves.

Having set up workshops in mathematics for low expectation pupils, the fourth stage might be for the co-ordinator to bring in examples of objectives approaches. Mathematics is probably the subject most suited to behavioural analysis. Each lesson could be defined in terms of precision teaching. The schemes of Kolstoe (1972), Ainscow and Tweddle (1979) and Aileen Duncan (1979) could each save teachers who were attempting to write curricula for bottom sets a great deal of time. Yet for teachers who have experienced what such groups can do with especially effective teaching, there are assumptions in each of these books that could be profitably questioned. Rather than simply accepting them, these books can be used as starting points for discussion. This is more likely to lead to the development of the autonomous professional we saw as nearest to the ideal of the special educator. In schools where the majority of mathematics staff are unlikely to stay with the workshops this long, the co-ordinator and the minority could then produce curricula based not merely on the individual and group profiles as they appear through assessment, but as what they think, as committed professionals discussing the problems informally among themselves, low expectation pupils could be capable of.

At the beginning of one upper school course in the author's school, the 40 children who had fared the worst in an internal examination were divided between two mathematics staff. One teacher spent most of the term giving his group arithmetic examples. The other developed a curriculum based mainly on geometry and social arithmetic, how to estimate miles per gallon and gas meter readings, for instance. Given sufficiently clear explanations, the second teacher found his groups could make good progress and that pupil understanding did not necessarily keep pace with the number of examples attempted. This is a very similar experience to the research finding of Soviet psychologists:

> It was experimentally confirmed that variations of form and positions alone, without the organizational strength of the teacher's explanations, does not foster the mastery of concepts. Only when the teacher's explanations play the leading role in induction does variation in geometric illustration help the pupil to abstract essential features and to master the true geometric relationship.
> (Zykovas: quoted in Kilpatrick & Wirsup: 1976)

It was obvious on entering the rooms which of the who groups was working harder and learning more. As it happened, we had given all 40 pupils one of the Schonell arithmetical tests at the beginning of the year (Schonell and Schonell: 1950). This appears to have limited practice effects and we retested the groups six months later. The author assisted in the administration of the test. The class which had pages of sums to its credit had actually regressed. Whilst we could make no claims for these results as an indicator of long term improvement, the class with the more adventurous curriculum and more cognitively and affectively sympathetic teacher made almost 0.5 of a year's progress.

Having started with extending the professional skills of the subject staff in such areas as reading, other aspects of language and mathematics, the fourth aspect of the co-ordinator's role is to encourage professional development within the teachers' own disciplines. A distinction may have to be drawn between the medium through which a body of knowledge is communicated and the specific demands each body of knowledge makes. Much can be done in departments through a successful Language Across the Curriculum group. We have already referred to the use of readability formulae and the Nottingham Reading for Learning project. However, language development policies often seem to fall short of the way departmental staff perceive the problems of low ability and troublesome children. Whilst it may be self apparent to a language specialist that one can not teach with an inadequate basis in communication and that this is a problem of great concern to the backward reader, the scientist, geographer or craft teacher may well see the reinforcement of the media of learning as an additional task. For many staff educational objectives are identified with their own particular form of knowledge.

A workshop session on teaching Science to low expectation pupils might raise the question: Why do it at all? The discipline could be conceived as a body of inter-related knowledge which itself requires firstly a tremendously wide and sound command of facts and secondly a method of generating and verifying hypotheses which also requires a highly developed sense of logic. By definition, the slow learner can be expected to have a poor memory and is often confined to concrete and intuitive levels of thinking. Science teaching to the full range of ability thus seems a cynical exercise in pseudo-egalitarianism. A discipline which ought to dispel prejudice and question dogma is reduced to a form of secular religion where pupils are made to take on trust facts whose significance they can never understand.

The only answer to such scepticism is that, given the right sort of encouragement and ingenuity, Science lessons can give low expectation pupils some insight into the range and methodology of the subject. As in the teaching of mathematics, the co-ordinator has to learn enough of the subject and to have taught it successfully to special classes before he can talk convincingly on the scientists' own ground. Examples may be given from the co-ordinator's experience of how pupils duplicated experiments in their own time. A lesson about hot air balloons and atmospheric pressure had encouraged one low expectation pupil to make his own at home and bring in an extensive piece of writing about it. Tape or video recordings of discussions in which 'slow learners' employed inferential and deductive thinking can be played and the problem of generating formal thought from concrete and intuitive responses discussed. A second stage can be to look at topics which seem to have worked with non-examination groups. Here again the co-ordinator may be swamped with ideas and methodologies from the higher reaches of the subject which could be re-examined from the perspective of the least able. One colleague had done a tongue-in-cheek project on Domestic Physics. Soap powders were weighed and their value for money estimated. Then they were tried out in the school's washing machine and the volume of bubbles per unit weight appraised. Lastly, dirty dishcloths were washed in them and optical instruments used to measure whiteness. Finally the whole experiment was written up in a group exercise as a parody of a washing powder advertisement and the result sent in with cartoons to the School Magazine.

As the third phase of these workshop sessions, the objectives approaches of Kolstoe (1972), Ainscow and Tweddle (1979) and Brennan (1979) could be discussed. It may be, however, that whilst the overt topic of such a discussion is curriculum development, the real problem may still be motivation and discipline. Some of the teachers may feel that while the remedial department and Head of Science may be able to teach low ability pupils, it is beyond them. In such a case, the Science teacher is thrown into the vicious cycle of cancelling laboratory time because of disruptive behaviour. The teacher's own sense of survival becomes the predominant issue in his relationship with alienated groups and a folklore develops that because of the glass, acid and other dangerous and expensive equipment, discipline in Science has to be impersonal and pre-emptive.

Whilst co-operating with the co-ordinator in the writing of a curriculum, the Science department may in fact feel that he has little real help to offer them. Special classes are almost invariably smaller than Science sets, there are less constraints in terms of CSE passes and so on. In this situation the role of the co-ordinator may well be to continue the curriculum evaluation in such a way as to allow less confident teachers to be more open in their discussion of such issues. In one school where the author worked, the Head of Science used the Socratic method of questioning and invited the pupils to find holes in his knowledge as a way of capturing their interest. When the author mentioned how successful such tactics could be, his response was that he had always done this and assumed his colleagues did so, too. In fact, quite a few of them had found class discussions so difficult they had retreated to dictated notes and harsh discipline. This only came into the open as a result of these informal curricular discussions.

The same role as catalyst may be employed with teachers of Craft subjects. Quite a few seem caught between the demand to make their subject more academically respectable, and the caretaker role with alienated older pupils. The examination syllabi make demands in terms of writing and technical expertise which would seem to exclude slow learners, and Craft teachers may themselves feel uneasy about them. Some may arrange a series of trivial unskilled jobs to keep such children occupied. All around them the average and able pupils do the real work, however. Fortunately there is an ideology, fuelled by some recent domestic science in-service courses, that these subjects have cognitive and affective dimensions which apply across the ability range, and this can be tapped by the co-ordinator. In the event of his possessing craft skills himself, for example in art, car maintenance and cookery, these can provide the basis for closer co-operation between special classes and mainstream teachers.

The fifth aspect of the co-ordinator's role, liaising with pastoral and counselling staff, external agencies, special schools, parents and employers, are discussed in later chapters since they are shared with those of the remedial education and special class teachers. The sixth aspect to which all the others are clearly related is the maintenance of caring and supportive ethos within the subject staff. For a range of educational and political reasons, the traditional isolation of the special class seems extremely dubious. In an economic situation where the teachers who do not generate good examination results in the core curriculum are especially vulnerable, the co-ordinator and other special education orientated staff ought to spend a proportion of their time teaching average and able children in their own subject speciality. Many reports of special units for disabled, partially hearing and sighted children (e.g. Jamieson, Parlett and Pocklington: 1977; Cope and Anderson: 1975, etc.) argue that the integration of these children could be made more difficult by the fact that mainstream teachers see so little of special unit staff. The remedial teacher in the outstandingly successful mining village schools mentioned above (page 24) was encouraged to put aside some of her time for coaching able readers. Remedial staff in other schools become sixth form tutors or take 'O' and 'A' level groups. It ought to be the ideal that in a comprehensive school, staff should be just as good at teaching 'A' level as remedial readers. Where Head of Remedial is a sinecure for semi-retired P.E. teachers, this reflects on the pupils. This is all the more reason for the co-ordinator to seek some involvement in mainstream work. Where there is a policy group for gifted children he might join this, too, since recommendations for small groups of high status pupils can well be turned to the advantage of the low expectation pupils too.

As a corollary of his examination work, his support of named teachers in subject departments and his other liaising, the co-ordinator needs to convince the Headteacher and staff that whilst his major concern is with low attaining and troublesome children, he has a commitment to the school as a whole. His objective is not to provide the school with a safety net, although this is a byproduct of his role; it is to utilize the professional resources within it, to reduce the sense of failure and to defeat the lowest expectations. He has an important in-service education role, training staff to teach language and mathematics skills, encouraging them to think more deeply about educational objectives and the interpersonal dimensions of achieving them.

To secure this trend, the co-ordinator must ensure that the Headteacher knows what he is doing and is personally involved in it. A start can be made by sending low expectation pupils to him so that he can see their work or hear their reading. He can be invited to watch the remedial or special class teacher at work. Finally, he may be asked to join the group of special staff who are helping to teach children to read. Given their role as arbiters of discipline, many Headteachers feel shy of exposing their authority to day to day teaching with what are potentially the most alienated groups in the school. Instead of taking a whole reading set, the Headteacher may prefer to start with an individual child. Success will make him much more confident about assessing the performance of subject staff with low expectation pupils. It may be that the real problem in teaching such children is the lack of power in the system that may be used on their behalf. Joyce Morris (1966) found that where primary school Headteachers are committed to the reading standards of the least able, they can have a distinctive effect. Whilst attitudes among comprehensive staff are likely to be considerably more disparate, it seems probable that the Headteacher's indifference would be reflected throughout the school.

The role of co-ordinator is one way for those involved with remedial education of special classes at middle management level to maximise the influence available to them. It rests on their own ability to get the best from low achieving and troublesome children, but it also incorporates the capacity to talk to a range of adults from a position of professional expertise in many areas of the curriculum. Like the Headteacher or deputy in charge of curriculum development, he must know a little about everything. His power base is not merely his personal qualities and his acceptance by alienated pupils, there must also be an esteem among a wider circle of staff, including the Headteacher.

Chapter Five

ISSUES OF SUPPORT AND CONTROL

Strong relationships with low expectation pupils and a commitment to the school as a whole could be seen as complimentary aims of a co-ordinated approach to special education. However, it has to be recognized that what seems to staff a kind of support can inadvertantly function as a form of social control. Some of the measures taken to alleviate the problems caused by disruptive non-examination pupils can inadvertantly reinforce their alienation and lower their educational and job expectations, as we have seen in the first chapter. It would be the main contention of this chapter that the strongest relationships open areas of conflict to joint staff-pupil exploration and allow pupils greater freedom in making decisions. This may well be done in a wider context than the special class and involve another kind of special teacher.

The emotional attributes of the slow learner have been a traditional concern of remedial education. Burt (1937) suggested that a proportion of educational backwardness was caused by 'conative' rather than cognitive factors. Certain children came to a 'standstill in their work' because of some 'shortage or leakage of moral energy or will'. While the full range of 'adult abnormalities' were not to be found in schools, there were 'temperamental defects' which the teacher could help to diagnose and treat. Burt clearly envisaged this area as one in which teachers and educational psychologists should work more closely.

Ablewhite (1967) found that when the remedial teachers in a post war secondary modern school began to develop a more open relationship with their classes, reading improved and rates of delinquency dropped. His classes were wary of discussion and it was only when they felt safe enough to say what they felt that their motivation improved. Programmes of social, emotional and vocational development played a large part in the thinking of Tansley and Gulliford (1960). They argued that slow learners are liable to be impulsive, lacking in self-control, inattentive, lazy or aggressive. What they needed was security, affection, acceptance by other children, independence and responsibility. Play, make believe and creative activities were thought to be of especial benefit. The rationale would appear to be that unless the ethos of a special class were mildly therapeutic, it would be unlikely to get the most from pupils educationally. In the remedial groups which Collins (1961) analysed at the University of Birmingham, the trainee psychologists aimed to make their work 'partly therapeutic', although as he points out, 'the situation in which they worked kept them teachers rather than psychotherapists'. Giving a new twist to this long-standing notion, the Somerset Psychologist, David Lawrence (1971) brought 'responsible, sympathetic adults' into 'four typical village schools in a rural community' to provide backward readers with counselling. Reading ages improved in the experimental group even when these adults took no part in the reading programme. Partly because it has been so difficult to determine what Lawrence meant by counselling, the experiment has proved hard to duplicate. Lawrence claims to have been 'influenced' by Rogers' 'Client Centred Therapy' (1951) but not to have used his 'techniques'. When a child expressed hostility towards a 'counsellor', Lawrence says he will 'very quickly be aware of the counsellor's attitudes towards whatever topic is under discussion'. This seems closer to the concepts of befriending and guidance than counselling in the Rogerian sense. The Bullock Committee appreciated the linguistic implications of Lawrence's work, however. It argued that retarded readers should be allowed 'regular informal conversation with sympathetic adults, not necessarily teachers'. The pupils might thereby 'regain confidence and show an increased capacity to learn' (H.M.S.O.: 1975: para. 18:15).

The Isle of Wight survey (Rutter, Tizard and Whitmore: 1970) put these issues in rather a different light. Firstly, it showed that there was little evidence that 'progress classes' contributed to their pupils' emotional development. This lends support to Collins's earlier finding about the remedial groups he researched (Collins: 1961). Secondly, the association between reading retardation and anti-social behaviour turned out to have been rather more complex than the therapeutic model suggested. Whilst reading problems seem in some cases to have followed from emotional difficulties, it also caused them in others. Rutter and Yule were clearly unprepared to relate their findings to the workings of schools and the relationship between schools and society in any depth. Yet they did argue that:

> The child who fails to read and who thereby falls behind in his school work may rebel against all the values associated with school when he finds he cannot succeed there. These school values include obedience to authority and respect for property.

Whilst this represents a somewhat mechanistic view of the development of values amongst poor readers, it does allow for the idea that the school context may itself generate problems as well as relieve them.

The third important finding of the Isle of Wight study was that there were children in school whose reading was adequate but who had 'psychiatric disorders'. The Isle of Wight team discarded the concept of maladjustment as circular, preferring 'psychiatric disorders'. This they defined as:

> Absormality of behaviour, emotions or relationships .. sufficiently marked and sufficiently prolonged to cause handicap to the child himself and/or distress and disturbance in the family or community.

Whilst this may have helped the research team to determine the attributes of the children, it 'ignores the context of the behaviour' as they themselves admitted. Insofar as reading failure may generate such 'abnormalities of behaviour' it would seem that the study missed a vital social-psychological dimension. The Warnock Committee simultaneously argued for the retention of the term 'maladjustment' whilst using Rutter and Yule's statistics in order to estimate the prevalence of special needs in this area. They were also rather vague about what the response of ordinary schools' staff should be. They suggest that 'special educational need' implies the need for 'particular attention to the social structure and emotional climate in which education takes place', and that:

> Ordinary schools vary widely in the degree to which they recognize and are able to cater for individual needs within their curriculum and organization.

Whilst seeming to allow the possibility that disciplinary problems, including those associated with school failure, may reflect on the organization of the school as a whole, such a suggestion sidesteps the issues raised by ten years of previous sociological work on delinquency and truancy. David Hargreaves (1968) had found that streaming itself contributes to a 'delinquescent' ethos among boys in a secondary modern school. In an MRC project, Power et al (1967) had shown that when delinquency rates in a socially homogeneous area of East London were compared, some schools had consistently higher rates than others. In six years:

> The low rate schools have hardly changed position: year after year they have only a few boys, if any, before the courts. The high rate schools have also shown little change over the years.

Power did find that there were neighbourhoods within his area that contributed much more adult crime than others, but that when these were taken into account 'there was little difference in the delinquency rates of boys coming from "high" or "low" districts'. Other factors like school size, age and type of school buildings, sex and ethnic composition and overall ability gradings were also discounted. The authors claimed that they have 'explained nothing' except that 'some schools seem to exert a positive and beneficent influence on the conduct of their pupils'.

In a study of absenteeism in South Wales, Reynolds (1976) found that good attendance was affected by organizational factors such as the enforement of uniform, and little caning. In a later article on the day to day disciplinary effectiveness of teachers, Reynolds (1977) argued that confrontative methods generated pupil problems, but where pupils were included in discussions of rules and situations and allowed to feel they had a meaningful role in the way a school ran, there were less.

Power intended to make a rather fuller study of these issues, but his original article created such controversy that the project was turned over to Rutter. He and his associates found (Rutter et al: 1979) that size of school, arrangements for mixed ability or streaming, the allocation of pastoral time, had no effect and that there was little relationship between in-school behaviour, examination successes, attendance rates and the pockets of high delinquency already described by Power. High rates of disciplinary intervention, particularly caning, correlated with poor pupil behaviour. Good group management and group based discipline had a good effect on work and behaviour, as did giving children responsibility and encouraging participation. Praise had a beneficial effect, provided that it was given on the spot. Poor teacher commitment, as in poor timekeeping, lack of discussion about courses, not putting the pupils' work on the walls, was also decisive. Where there was a counsellor, this contributed to a larger degree of informal discussion between teachers and troubled children.

Rutter's evidence would indicate that when this enlarged concept of special educational provision is considered, the management and ethos of the school community are of as much concern as the treatment of individuals and small groups. It is even debated whether small groups for low attainers necessarily help pupils' attitudes (Cashdan, Pumfrey and Lunzer: 1971; Summers and Woolf: 1977). Elizabeth Jones found (Barton and Tomlinson: 1982) that when very difficult children were sent to a resource room mainly used by children with moderate learning difficulties and physical handicaps, they were met with a largely negative response. It may be that, as the author found, a great deal of the effectiveness of special provision depends on the relationship that the given teacher can establish with specific pupils, even when these teachers were chosen from among the most sympathetic on the staff. Where, as a lukewarm approach to co-ordination could take place, staff are chosen on the basis of their inefficiency within their own departments, the results could be worse than conventional remedial education.

Many remedial teachers, including the author, have become involved in counselling children with emotional or behavioural difficulties, whatever their educational attainments. Rutter clearly hoped that children in ordinary schools with 'psychiatric disorders' would benefit from seeing professionals other than psychiatrists:

> Nor is there any implication that psychiatrists are necessarily the appropriate therapists for these children.

However, as his review of the literature indicates, Rutter was well aware of the limitations of counselling, whether performed by trained psychiatrists or lay people. Eysenck (1952) and Shepherd et al (1966) showed that children referred to Child Guidance fared no better than untreated children. After reviewing the way clients, their families and counsellors perceived treatment, Truax and Carkhuff (1967) were forced to accept that:

> Eysenck was essentially correct in saying that the average counselling and psychotherapy as it is currently practised does not result in average client improvement greater than that observed in clients who receive no counselling or psychotherapeutic treatment.

Success rates varied between 91 per cent in 78 cases to 42 per cent in 191 cases. Truax and Carkhuff found some clients who felt that they had been harmed by the experience. Some counsellors seemed to have remarkably little insight into their clients' feelings and these were often preoccupied with their own roles as therapists. In another critical view of counselling, Arbuckle (1975) found that instead of putting the child's view of ethics first, many school counsellors 'still believe that somehow, in some way values can be taught'. Carkhuff and Berenson (1977) argued that the therapists' personal qualities were much more significant than length or orientation of training and this has been substantiated in subsequent research.

In a review article entitled 'Does Anything Work?' Joel Fischer (1978) argues that:

> The evidence is clear that psychotherapy is not uniformly effective. Although the research does suggest that psychotherapy or some aspect thereof can be effective, the current state of the literature does not provide a clear answer as to whether or not the positive benefits are sufficient to outweigh the negative side effects and investment of time, energy and financial resources that also ensue.

He also pointed out that there is a substantial body of research 'illustrating the significant and positive effects of the communication of the interpersonal skills of empathy, warmth and genuineness on a range of client and student behaviours'.

Issues of Support and Control

If the role of counsellor may in itself be of little use or even harmful, there are additional difficulties for a counsellor who spends part of his week also working as a remedial teacher. Having dispensed eith the ritualized distance of teacher-pupil relationships in one setting, it may prove difficult to operate without it in others. One teacher-counsellor caught in such a dilemma was nicknamed 'Blue Band' by one remedial class because of the slogan that this kind of margarine 'spread soft straight from the fridge'. Carl Rogers himself had few illusions about the authoritarian structures in our schools and society:

> Since our culture to a very large degree is organized on an authoritarian and hierarchical basis and only partly on a democratic basis, it may seem to some that education should reflect that ambivalence. Each must reach his own conclusions.

There seems little doubt that where 'abnormalities of behaviour, emotions or relationships' are concerned, behaviour modification represents the more reliable 'treatment'. Fischer's review article refers to over 150 published rigorous case studies 'using the ABAB reversal design .. (which shows) .. that the technique or program per se is responsible for the change'. In Britain too there seems to have been a move away from the Educational Psychologist as therapist, towards a teacher advisor in the use of behaviourist techniques (Gillham: 1978). There has been considerable resistance to this from teaching staffs however (Wheldall: 1980). There seem to be four major reasons for this. Firstly, teachers seem to feel that it dilutes their personal authority. Secondly, positive reinforcement appears to amount to bribery. Thirdly, it may be felt that whilst it may not necessarily be used to produce mechanical or conformist behaviour, this is its most likely function. Fourthly, when extrinsic reinforcers are withdrawn, abnormal behaviours may start to recur. Fischer concluded that the best hope for long term success was a range of techniques and personal qualities including behaviour modification and the Rogerian virtues of warmth and congruence.

behaviour modification

This balanced and comprehensive article has important implications for the remedial and special class teacher concerned about the effects of lowered expectations and the social control of low attaining working class children. If there are pupils referred for small group treatment who do not respond to offers of help and who may thereby become labelled as beyond anything the ordinary school can do, behaviour modification may represent the lesser of two evils. Clifford, for instance, went through a period in the fourth year where his behaviour became intolerable for most members of staff. He persisted in whistling and shouting out in lessons, defying teachers and threatening those who tried to hit him. He had always been a difficult child but his behaviour had become much more disruptive. Sending the child to the Headteacher and counselling had had little positive effect and the staff needed more help in coping with him. The alternative was suspension or transfer to a special unit. The role of the special education teacher was used to co-ordinate a meeting of all the teachers concerned and work out what aspects of his behaviour were most difficult for them. Eight target behaviours were decided upon by the staff and it was agreed to send him out of the room for 'time out' at any instances of these negative behaviours and pay him a reward of 2p per lesson where good behaviour and hard work were in evidence. Whilst this programme was in operation, Clifford's behaviour was transformed. Later the defiance and shouting began to recur, but the crisis had passed and there was no further danger of exclusion.

In the last few weeks of the fifth year when the non-examination group was baulking at the prospect of school work, yet feeling there was little point in coming to school without it, a token economy was set up. Ayllon and Azrin (1960) discovered that in an institution where a large number of people evinced antisocial behaviour, it was possible to reinforce desired behaviours by regular payment of tokens which could be redeemed later. Under guidance from the Educational Psychologist, a points system was grafted into lessons. At regular periods during writing or silent reading lessons, all the pupils who were concentrating on their work received two points - one for working and one for not disrupting anyone else. Those who were not working but who were quiet received one point and those who were talking and not working were ignored. This led to a much higher level of concentration. Some played the system at first and only put pen to paper at the moment the points were given out; others tried to ignore the teacher but most accepted it, as these comments from the group showed:

> Dave: I like to start this lesson straight away 'cos I can get more points at the end. And we go fishing at the weekend.
>
> Pat: The points system's good. It means you (i.e. the teacher) don't have to be so nasty.

Winett and Winckler (1972) show that behaviour modification does not need to be used merely to attain passive 'seat work' behaviours. During a discussion or drama lesson 'adult behaviour' would be reinforced. Rules for what constituted 'adult behaviour' could be redefined by a group decision. Pupils who were normally shy might receive two tokens for contributing to a discussion while extroverts might be rewarded for thinking before they spoke or letting others talk. From time to time there would be group meetings about how the points earned could be spent, on fishing or swimming trips or on biscuits. Gifts of time or sweet things may be used by teachers to unfreeze difficult relationships and it could be argued that warmth and openness are all that is necessary to prompt adult behaviour in school leavers' groups. Yet there are situations where the power of a good relationship may be insufficient to break through hardened expectations. In this case behaviour modification can be a positive alternative.

Just as the co-ordinator has brought together staff who are especially good at teaching low attaining pupils for reading tuition, so he could enhance the skills of teachers who are especially gifted in their relations with antisocial or withdrawn pupils. These could be drawn together on the same basis as the reading tutors, according to the children's recommendations. There is a grapevine in schools about which teachers can be approached, which ask unhelpful questions and which gossip in the staffroom. Not all the children want to talk to the same teacher and the author found that the existence of a counsellor encouraged contacts between unhappy children and a wider circle of staff.

Although there are similarities in the development of this kind of support group and the curriculum groups already mentioned, ideas and information play a secondary role in the development of interpersonal skills. A start can be made in schools. There may be a series of seminars where educational psychologists, social workers and the school counsellor talk about casework skills. Particularly difficult children could be chosen for case study discussion. Where there are strong links with outside agencies, these could be invited to supply a chairman.

Support groups could take on a much stronger role if members were to go on training courses outside school, however. The National Marriage Guidance Council run introductions to counselling in different parts of the country and there are WEA courses on Group Dynamics and Counselling. For the school teacher, one of the orientations with particular relevance is Transactional Analysis or T.A., and as this has some useful things to say about the role of adults in situations of conflict, it is discussed in some detail below.

Eric Berne developed the approach to ego psychology basic to T.A. in a book called 'The Games People Play' (1978). He suggested three different aspects to the personality: parent, adult and child. In this system, the parent is seen as part critical authority, part nurturent support. The adult is devoid of emotion, logical and dispassionate. The child may be inventive, spontaneous, intuitive or demonic. Each grown up has all three parts of this personality system and he learns about the identities of these three aspects in childhood. It is thought that a person's 'script', or the way he views his role in life, is laid down before the age of seven and that we are largely unaware of the power of these early childhood fantasies. Hence our view of how the 'parent' should act may be coloured by the way we saw our parents acting when we were young. All through life, we get ourselves into situations which are 'not OK' and it is through using our 'adult' and dispassionately analyzing them that we can 'update' our views of ourselves and others. The same relationship may bring out different aspects of these ego states. For instance, the beginning mathematics teacher may think of his subject in logical terms without emotional involvement, so he might attempt to engage his class from his 'adult'. Where the children are successful and well motivated, they will put their 'mischievous child' into abeyance and respond from their 'adults' too. There will be a mutually satisfactory lesson in which the teacher teaches, the children learn and there is a rational, academic atmosphere in the class. Where the pupils are unsuccessful and feel 'not OK' about their mathematics, a new range of ego states will be called into play. The pupils may respond to the teacher's logical dispassionate air by inventively testing out the teacher's authority. One or two of the children may be demonically mischievous. The teacher responds from his 'critical parent', telling the pupils what kind of behaviour he expects of them and warning them to conform. With a particularly alienated group this might have little effect and the teacher experiences fear and confusion. Without realizing it, he too has switched into his 'child' state. Teacher and pupils are now set to play the well-known game of 'mayhem'. The overt object of the lesson may well be to teach a certain mathematics topic, but both teacher and class know that the real excitement is in provoking the teacher to lose his temper, make wild threats and so on. Both sides are in the grip of an infantile fantasy about 'schools' which can be seen just as clearly whenever primary pupils play 'school' in a drama lesson.

For the teacher to get out of such a situation he must first become aware of it through his 'adult'. Blaming the children, attempting to punish them into submission, reporting the most disruptive children to the pastoral tutor or counsellor simply sidesteps his problem. He may well want to teach these pupils but they for their part are full of childish fears and inhibitions. Rather than take the risk and experience fresh failure, they disrupt his programme. The teacher now has to refer to that part of his own personality which is inventive and intuitive - his child. He may suspect that if only he could get them to relax and accept him, he could make some of those intellectual risks more tolerable. So he might choose to start his lesson with an informal chat rather than a lecture, letting the group know he is in a good mood and ready for a few laughs before the real work begins. By going on a T.A. course, the teacher learns how to unbend and how to appear warmer and more friendly to others. Having started to develop a closer interpersonal bond, he may now talk to the group from his nurturent parent, encouraging them to try out difficult material, helping them when they want to give up, administering praise for every success. On the T.A. course, the teacher might also learn that when he thinks he is being 'nurturent', others perceive him as 'critical'. Such a revelation is painful, but such groups are generally warm and supportive.

Issues of Support and Control

Praise and many other aspects of interpersonal contact are known in T.A. parlance as 'strokes'. Strokes can be of four kinds: OK, OK conditional, not OK and not OK conditional. 'OK' and 'not OK' strokes are directed at the person. For instance, when the teacher says 'hello' to a child and communicates that he likes him, that is an 'OK' stroke. When he scowls or deliberately discounts what someone is trying to tell him that is a 'not OK' stroke. Conditional strokes concern contingencies rather than personalities. The teacher may congratulate a child on his work or he may be cross because a child was out of his seat. Neither teacher nor child will feel there is anything of great personal weight attached to these interactions. Most teachers operate a balance between 'conditional OK' and 'conditional not OK' strokes with occasional 'OK' and 'not OK' strokes. The T.A. group may be a place where this sort of balance can be analysed. Even quite successful teachers may find that there are far more 'conditional not OK' strokes than 'OK' and 'conditional OK'. Taking a notebook and dividing a sheet into four columns, they tick off each of their contacts over a ten minute session. With pupils who are particularly quiet or disruptive, they can run an individual profile. Having used one's 'adult' to analyse the problem, the 'child' is brought into play. There is an effort to develop a genuine but friendly state of mind towards the child or group. The T.A. training session may provide a setting where this can be discussed, then the pattern of interaction can be 'updated'.

T.A. can be of direct help in informal conversations with unhappy children or those who are locked into confrontations at school. Janet was a bright underachieving girl whose mother informed the school that she had taken an overdose. Janet was fifteen. She wanted to leave school, get a job and marry her boyfriend, but there had been arguments at home. Her parents had found out that she had been sleeping with her boyfriend and had tried to put a stop to the relationship. Janet knew her mother and grandmother had been engaged at fifteen and married at sixteen and she had felt that she should be allowed to, also. Her mother had left school by that age, got a job and saved up some money before she was married. She thought Janet was being irresponsible. All that Janet could see was that her mother (like most of her teachers) was treating her like a child, whilst she felt she was an adult. On a one to one basis, these interpersonal difficulties were clarified and the pressures alleviated.

William was an even more intelligent fifteen year old. He seemed to be taking less interest in his 'O' levels. He was refusing to do any homework and he announced that he wanted to leave at Easter. It emerged that his father had been the only boy from his working class estate to have gone to grammar school. When all his peers had left school and gone to work he had lost heart. Later he had joined the Navy and that helped him regain faith in himself. William wanted to join the Marines, for which he did not need 'O' levels. Informal discussion with the school counsellor helped William to look at the problems of breaking ranks with family and friends and his own fantasies about his role in life more objectively. He could now make a decision based on an updated view of himself. That is not to say that the teacher is attempting 'to teach values'. The conflicts represented by this kind of situation would anyway seem insoluble in our society. In the relationship where the pupil trusts the teacher enough to talk to him about such a problem, the teacher has to reflect the pupil's own sense of ethics. In this case William worked hard enough to gain two 'O' levels and left immediately after the examinations. This was still considerably less than some staff thought him capable of, although it was more 'realistic' than his original intention.

The chief value of such training courses, so far as a co-ordinated view of special educational provision is concerned, is that it allows groups of staff who have been on them together to develop more open, trusting relationships among themselves. Case study seminars, informal staffroom conversations and weekend visits with alienated children take on a new meaning when staff feel they can rely more deeply on one another. It is even possible to forestall the kind of scapegoating of low expectation and deviant pupils that seems to occur in staffrooms. Hargreaves et al (1975) and Woods (1979) refer to the processes whereby the 'biographies' of difficult pupils are built up through staff gossip. When dealing with children who transgress normal expectations, teachers may label them as a way of managing their own uncertainties. Such a label might crystalize and take on a life of its own. A support group can question the appropriateness of such labels by presenting a more positive view of the pupils. This could result in a more constructive attitude in the staff as a whole.

This kind of shift in attitudes, grounded in the experience of a minority of sympathetic staff, with a common awareness of skills like T.A. and counselling, may help to bring about a more 'incorporative ethos' within the school. Many teachers find that discussing school rules with their classes helps the children to feel more of a stake in the way the school runs. The author has set up experiments in group couselling whereby a whole class looks at a particular problem dispassionately through discussion and role play. One class contained a boy called Daniel who was being considered for suspension or transfer to a special school. In a previous lesson they had got completely out of hand. Daniel had become involved in a fight with the teacher which ended with the teacher being pushed out of the classroom. In the afternoon lesson the class told the author what had happened, how provoked Daniel had been and how they would all now be in trouble.

There was an obvious clash of loyalties involved. On the one hand the colleague needed to be given support. On the other, there was a child whose 'behavioural abnormalities' were being exacerbated by unfortunate handling and the rest of the class's behaviour. Roleplay seemed to present an opportunity to reassert social control on behalf of the authorities and to enable the children to understand how best to keep Daniel out of trouble. They were invited to re-enact the morning's lesson, except that Daniel and the other teacher would be 'played' by two other children. Daniel and the author took the roles of directors. The morning's drama was gradually re-created and from time to time the author stopped the performance to ask Daniel and the other pupils whether what they were doing was true to life. Where they thought it was silly or exaggerated, the scene was replayed.

Each time the roleplay was interrupted, pupils and teacher discussed why the various incidents happened and what had been going on in the original actors' minds. The class knew intuitively that although Daniel had been terribly behaved, he was only doing what many of them would like to have done. Just because they had not pushed the teacher, it did not mean to say they were innocent. Their own raucous behaviour had added to the strain on the teacher, which had contributed to the confrontation with Daniel. They had been told about the concept of corporate responsibility by teachers before, but for most of them the idea did not mean very much. After the roleplay and discussion, they began to understand that if Daniel were suspended because of the incident, they too had a responsibility. At this point they were ready to discuss ways in which they could keep Daniel out of further trouble. Daniel was not bad in everyone's lesson, but in those which brought out the worst in him, the class could help to keep him out of the limelight.

'Lessons' like these where pupils show themselves as they really behave, make a vivid impression on both the 'deviant' pupils and their 'innocent' classmates. Some pupils from this particular class were still talking about the effect it had had on them four years later as they prepared to take up courses in University and Teacher Training Colleges. With Daniel, the experiment had come too late. He was transferred to a neighbouring school shortly afterwards and was eventually excluded permanently. Despite the intention to reconcile the needs of the system and those of the pupils, it may appear to colleagues that such activities go too far in contravening basic professional loyalties, however, and the support group must beware of a hardening of feeling amongst more conventional staff.

Where there is a sufficiently strong support group within the staff, willing to take a more questioning view of deviance, the notion of a special class operating as a sanctuary becomes less plausible. There are pupils on the verge of leaving school who continue to demand the security, affection and acceptance which Tansley and Gulliford argued special classes and schools ought to provide (Tansley and Gulliford: 1960). It may be that in some schools a special class is the only way in which disruptive low attainers can be contained. But where there are five or six staff in fourth and fifth year options who possess the personal resources to calm children down, motivate them and give their colleagues support during bad patches, the 'deviant' pupils might be better off in an open setting than in a special class. Putting a group of disruptive pupils together can hardly help their self image. This might be particularly important when one considers that the highest delinquency rates occur in the year before leaving school.

Teachers forming such groups run risks. They are isolated from the conventional disciplinary ethos of the school and may not expect support from it in times of stress. Discussions with the pupils about the nature of discipline may make some colleagues feel that they are siding with the bad pupils against the teachers and, having found one adult on whom they can rely, some pupils may be relentless in their demands.

In this last situation it may be useful to develop strong links with the educational psychologist or social worker attached to the school. A teacher first asks the pupil's permission to break confidentiality. It may be emphasized that no names will be mentioned but that just as the teacher wants to help the pupil so this other adult is there to help the teacher. One colleague, Ms. Green, was working with a girl called Margaret who was unhappy at home and very lonely. She saw Margaret on a regular basis for half an hour a week and there were lots of opportunities for short chats and friendly exchanges during the week. The relationship meant a lot to Margaret and as it deepened she started visiting Ms. Green's flat. Gradually the visits lasted longer and took place two or three nights a week. The teacher was beginning to have no private life and was anxious about the girl's feelings for her. It would have been deeply threatening to talk to her colleagues at school about this and confidentiality would be infringed, anyway. At this point, she arranged a meeting with the psychologist. The psychologist reflected back to the teacher that while she could handle the relationship, it was time to set bounds to it. Reassured, Ms. Green told Margaret that she could only visit one night a week, without putting the pupil's feelings to the test.

Another child called Robert with whom the author had developed a strong relationship and who supposedly was a low attainer with an extraordinarily poor mathematical and spatial ability, became overwhelmed by his sense of anger and used to glower threateningly through his sessions. The psychologist suggested that the boy's language could not express all he felt and that other media might help. When drawing materials were brought in the boy, who had previously shown no artistic talents, drew a portrait of the author, full of feeling and objectivity.

The research literature would imply that in a field where hardly any approaches have a reliable chance of long term effectiveness, those operating them should have definite criteria of success. Rates of suspension or transfer to special schools, units and community homes might help. There would probably be a number of variables at work over which teachers might have little control, like placement availability, L.E.A. policy and Headteachers' attitudes, but long range trends within a given school might be some kind of indication. Power's delinquency rate - the proportion of convictions per hundred of the school population - ought to be another reasonable guide. Truax and Carkhuff (1967) would argue that pupils' beliefs should be considered. They might feel that the relationship or course of behaviour modification made a positive difference; or that the crisis would have passed anyway; or that it made life more difficult for them. As for the majority of pupils never seriously threatened by the mechanisms of social control, one would want to know whether lessons taught by the support group were more vital and 'incorporative' or whether they were no different from any other.

Recent developments in criminology and social psychology tend to throw into doubt concepts like 'disruptiveness', 'delinquency' and 'prevalence of antisocial pupils'. They re-emphasize the day to day relationships between people in authority, like the police and the teachers, and the community as a whole. It would be a fundamental tenet of labelling theory that whilst each society or social institution has beliefs about what constitutes normal or abnormal behaviour, individuals within them vary greatly in their responses to them. These variations can affect the numbers of deviants labelled. Some teachers are capable of making some children act in more intolerable ways, others are more tolerant themselves and a few seem to be able to help some children to survive the pressures of the system. It could be hoped that the support groups discussed in this chapter could effect the perception and the kinds of behaviour in schools, enabling them to integrate more children who are unhappy or who are in danger of being labelled disruptive, psychiatrically disordered or maladjusted.

Chapter Six

SPECIAL EDUCATION AND THE OUTSIDE AGENCIES

However useful Educational Psychologists may be in sustaining children with educational and behavioural difficulties in ordinary schools, it must not be forgotten that one of their most long-standing and important functions is to adjudicate in the transfer of such children to special schools. As such, this outside agency also becomes involved in issues of support and control. Whilst the Warnock Committee itself recommends the greater involvement of psychologists in preventative liaison work, Tomlinson (1981) and other sociologists have argued that their main concern was to arbitrate between the claims of the rival professional groups in the labelling process. So far as the pattern of transfer of children from ordinary to special schools was concerned, the pattern was originally laid down by the Departmental Committee on Defective and Epileptic Children (H.M.S.O.: 1898). Many of the witnesses were Medical Officers and when Kerr, the Medical Officer for Bradford, was asked about the advisability of medical intervention, he replied:

> It is essential I think. If it was left to the teachers, the teachers would try to get rid of all the dull children. They try to pass them through their hands.

Some of the witnesses, like Francis Warner, the Medical Officer for London, would have preferred provision to be made in terms of epidemiological surveys and transfers in terms of medical screening. Despite the scepticism of the teachers on the Committee about the efficacy of medical data in making educational decisions, it established that the initiative for a referral should rest with Headteachers and HMIs, but that a medical certificate should provide the legal basis for transfer. This was preserved in the H.P.1 until 1975 and the S.E.5 since.

Cyril Burt clearly wanted to involve class teachers and educational psychologists much more closely and Tansley and Gulliford (1960) proposed a thorough diagnosis by representatives of all professions, with the main examination in the hands of the psychologists:

> Whatever steps are taken to discover the children who may need special schooling, the next step should be a thorough diagnostic examination. The examination should be sufficiently comprehensive to reveal the causes of mental subnormality. It will take into consideration the child's physical, mental and educational status, his life history, his family background and other environmental influences to which he has been exposed. It therefore requires the co-ordinated efforts of doctors, teachers, psychologists and social workers .. The examination is preferably undertaken by a trained educational psychologist since the emphasis is on the child's educable capacity and requires not only knowledge about the interpretation of test scores, but also about schools and the educational process.

This degree of optimism about a psychologist's objectivity and expertise was reinforced by the Summerfield report on their training. Commenting on it, Philips (1970) argued that whilst professionals from a number of fields employed psychological knowledge, educational psychologists had a unique role. Theirs was to carry out assessments of children 'who are thought to have problems of learning and adjustment', to communicate 'the findings to parents, teachers and children in such a way as to improve their conception of the problem' and to produce what he calls 'therapeutic interventions through remedial help, child guidance or removal to special schools'. Until 1975 it was still possible for the medical officer to complete 2HP without reference to school, parents or educational psychologist, and then fill out the official certification.

Circular 2/75 made multi professional assessment the administrative basis of transfer. The Warnock Report envisaged this as a staged operation. At first the Headteacher must see what can be done within the confines of the school. Secondly, the Headteacher should consult a teacher with expertise and training in special education. Thirdly, there should be informal consultations with specialists from medicine, teachers of the blind and deaf, Child Guidance and Social Services. Only if these measures failed to solve the problem as the Headteacher sees it, should formal assessment begin. Form SE1, which comprises questions of attainment and educational difficulties, should be filled in by the Headteacher or a representative of his from the staff. Form SE2 asks questions about medical disabilities and is to be filled in by the Medical Officer. Form SE3 asks for a summary of attainments and behaviour and is to be filled in by the psychologist. Form SE4 is a summary of action and is to be filled in by representatives of the LEA and an experienced psychologist. Much to the irritation of many psychologists, the old medical certificate is still preserved as the SE5 and it is quite possible for the Medical Officer to overturn previous recommendations. Whilst Medical Officers still make many recommendations for children under 5 and have a theoretical power to impose transfer decisions, the administrative responsibility of the Schools Psychological Service has been considerably enlarged.

Just how therapeutic psychologists' interventions are has come under scrutiny recently. Removal to special schools or units would not always seem to be in the child's interests. Cope and Anderson's (1975) review of the integration of physically handicapped children found they made greater academic gains and had fewer emotional and adjustment difficulties. Jamieson, Parlett and Pocklington's (1978) evaluation of integration for the partially sighted found that although underachievement existed and there were rather more adjustment problems than teachers or parents knew about, it was preferred and produced better results. One of the implications of their study was that so much depended on the 'micro milieux' created by the teacher that success might be difficult to predict. G.W. Davies's (1981) unpublished dissertation, already referred to, found less 'maladjustment' but poorer academic achievements in ESN schools than in children with equivalent IQs in ordinary schools. Rutter, Tizard and Whitmore's Isle of Wight survey (1970: op cit) was even more critical of their ESN schools than their 'progress classes'. When the reading progress of the 'intellectually retarded' children in ordinary schools was compared with the same in ESN schools, it was 'considerably better':

> If a non reader is defined as someone who fails to score on a Neale Test, then it is found that none of the intellectually retarded children fall into that category but over half the children at the special school do.

It could be argued that there were other reasons for segregating children than low IQ. These may have continued to subvert reading progress after transfer to ESN schools. The only satisfactory way of evaluating segregation is to do as the American researchers, Goldstein, Moss and Jordan, did in 1965. They divided target children on a random basis between ordinary and special classes and despite the training given to special class teachers by the team, the academic attainments in the special class were still largely worse. Rutter argues that without comparison to <u>satisfactory</u> provision in ordinary schools, a full evaluation could not be made. He did express scepticism about the value of transfer, however:

> It is not surprising that some parents feel that a dreadful decision has been made concerning their child and consequently feel resentful.

Special Education and the Outside Agencies

In analyzing the role of community psychologists and psychiatrists, Szasz (1970) argued that their prime function was the 'warehousing' of eccentric, unusual and troublesome individuals. Some recently trained British psychologists would be equally concerned about becoming part of a:

> Ministry of Adjustment; however sophisticated its staff may be about psychodynamics, its basic interests will be in the kind of problem the student creates for the school and other people. This will serve as the real basis for classifying him and disposing of his case.

This is not to say that integration always works in the child's interests, however. Recent evaluation of the wholesale American programmes reveal a number of caveats. Many teachers have negative feelings towards handicapped children and as time goes by these intensify (Shotel, Iano and McGettigan: 1972). Agard (1975) found regular class teachers using inappropriate teaching strategies; Gickling and Theobold (1975) that 85 per cent felt they lacked the necessary skills. Jones et al (1978) concluded:

> Whether or not a teacher will provide an appropriate educational programme for a handicapped child depends on a number of factors including the teacher's self perceived ability to teach a particular child, the extent to which the handicapped child deviates from the modal performance level of the class and the teacher's attitude to that child.

The social psychology of the labelling process is so complex that it is difficult for psychologists to be sure which setting will be in a particular child's interests. They may not know enough in detail about specific teacher attitudes, classroom interaction or overall school organization. At present many lack the time to observe children in the full range of school activities, especially in secondary schools where pupils may have eight or more teachers. Despite the recommendations of the Warnock Report, Chazan et al (1980) found that many were not orientated to do so even with young children:

> The function of the Educational Psychologists seemed to be more to get children out of the nurseries and into special units than to help solve the problems they posed within the nurseries.

Gregory (1980) argues that in their hurried acceptance of a Headteacher or classteacher's account of a child's special educational needs, psychologists naively collude with schools' disciplinary structures. He quotes the case of a boy referred as a behaviour problem by his junior school. On further investigation it appeared that the teacher was new to this downtown school and was having great difficulties keeping order. At least eight other children were just as disruptive and Gregory concludes:

> Psychologists may be inadvertantly not only covering up inadequacies in school organization, as illustrated above, but camouflaging defects in educational policy.

The Co-ordinator of Special Education who has established good links with outside agencies as a support for the support group may find an additional problem when pupils are officially referred by the Headteacher. Jim had had befriending and remedial help through much of his school life and his position had been discussed on an informal basis with the psychologist. There had been a number of petty offences involving small thefts and riding a motor cycle underage and he was known to Social Services because of an Intermediate Treatment order. At the end of the Christmas term of his fifth year he was entered for CSE mock examinations. He did not want to stay on after Easter anyway, but his attainments in most subjects were so poor as to make the whole exercise humiliating. In company with other similarly frustrated pupils, he played up in an examination. He was now challenging a central principle in the educational ideology of the school. All pupils must have a chance to show how well they can do in examinations. He had also subverted its social control. There was a regular liaison meeting between the Headteacher, Educational Psychologist, Social Worker and Education Welfare Officer and in the course of it, Jim's progress was discussed. He was well known to all the officials and his apparent unregeneracy helped the Headteacher to organize his removal.

Such episodes raise the question about whether there can ever be a 'good' referral to the psychologist. Even at an informal level, this may make certain pupils more 'visible' and hence more liable to removal to a special school or disruptive unit whose provisions might be no improvement on the ordinary one. Not only do few psychologists observe children's behaviour in their ordinary schools, few Headteachers of ordinary schools know much about day to day work and interaction in special schools. One way out of this dilemma is for the co-ordinator himself to get to know his local special schools more thoroughly. A morning's visit may be enough for the co-ordinator to exchange ideas, but more prolonged observation and even a degree of teaching might be more useful. A list of curricular objectives, the results of criteria referenced testing and an outline of schemes used may look very impressive in the Headteacher's study. In order to evaluate their effectiveness, one needs to see them in relation to the school's hidden curriculum. For secondary school teachers, the last half term of the summer term, when the fifth year have left, may free mornings or afternoons for working in day special schools. Community homes and residential schools often welcome staff during the summer holidays and a week's stay, preferably residential so as to gain some insight into the inter-relationship of 'care' and education, may give the co-ordinator a more faithful impression that the psychologist's well announced visits allow.

Where individual children prove extremely troublesome, but the likely special school or disruptive unit does not appear to be in the child's interests, there is much a co-ordinator can do to calm the situation. An eleven year old boy called Peter had found the transfer from primary school unsettling. He had been obstreperous to two or three experienced members of staff. His older brothers and sisters had proved extremely difficult and home circumstances were harsh. His reading age was more than four years retarded and he failed to score on a group IQ test. There would seem to have been substantial prima facie grounds for referral. However, in the last year of the primary school he had made a strong relationship with the Deputy Headteacher with whom he had made good progress in reading. There was a form tutor in the comprehensive school who had taken a special interest in him. Although he was in the bottom mathematics set, his teacher found his mental arithmetic and attitude very good. If he was to have any chance of settling there had to be an alternative to the biography being constructed in the staffroom and in the Headteacher's mind. It emerged that the boy had extremely poor co-ordination and was subject to fits as a child and the psychologist was persuaded to make a referral to the paediatrician. Although the details were kept strictly confidential, the staff took a more sympathetic attitude, seeing the problem as 'medical' rather than 'behavioural'. It took almost a year for the child to be seen, during which time his reading and attitude improved and his appearance smartened up. After discovering a number of minor ailments and toying with the notion of Klinefelter's Syndrome, the paediatrician pronounced the boy normal. Epilepsy was ruled out and rugby prescribed for his obesity. Whilst it may have been risky to have called in a psychologist and a doctor, the prestige of a medical diagnosis had first delayed a decision and then underlined the pupil's normality. If medical decisions have been used to transfer children, with very little understanding of the educational issues, it might be wise for the co-ordinator of special schools to familiarize himself with the medical aspects of integration.

Despite calls for closer liaison between schools and social workers, the Warnock Committee's S.E. procedure suggests that the professional claims of social workers were discounted. This may or may not reflect current evaluative research. Fischer's (1976: 1978 op cit) is grim. In a review of seventeen American studies which subjected fully trained professionals to a thorough experimental design, he found that whatever the orientation, type of client or criteria of success, there is no evidence that they produced:

> Results superior to no treatment at all or in any way better than the minimal services provided by non-professional workers to a contrast group of clients.

Some professionals helped certain combinations of clients, but twelve of Fischer's studies provided evidence of relative deterioration in clients in the experimental groups.

There is a strong tradition in American criminology that social work might reinforce delinquency. Tannenbaum (1938) suggested:

> The first dramatization of the evil which separates a child out of his group for specialized treatment plays a greater role in making the criminal than perhaps any other experience.

In his analysis of the 'Child Savers', Platt (1964) argues that court officials and social workers have a professional interest in sustaining the flow of offenders and a predisposition to define behaviour which conflicted with their own middle class, anti-urban, Protestant values as delinquent. Patrick (1971) found that in certain respects, Glasgow social workers had little understanding of gang members' habits. Some were released from Approved Schools and Borstals in time to meet their mates on a Friday night. Employment was arranged in areas which meant they had to cross other gangs' territories. Community workers who kept them occupied at weekends and early evenings failed to realize that much of the theft and violence started much later on.

Lofland (1969) differentiated between 'normal smithing' and 'deviance smithing'. He argued that groups like Alcoholics Anonymous and certain members of the clergy and Salvation Army who put themselves 'on the line' to their clients at any time were much more liable to succeed than the nine-to-five social worker with his family commitments and short term intervention. It would seem in this country that with the increasing rise in the divorce rate and the promised trend towards non-custodial treatment of young offenders, there will be a growing formal commitment to case work among school children and their families. If local authorities reduce social service manpower, the quality of this provision is likely to be impoverished. A school counsellor or befriender may see more of a child and know his parents better than a case worker, anyway, and social work departments may well appreciate closer liaison with a school which has an effective special educational provision.

For their part, teachers may gain from watching effective community workers and C.S.V. staff at work on Intermediate Treatment placements. Here again, the chance to join a group on a residential basis might allow the befriender to see different sides of the child. Children placed on a residential care order may miss a well-liked teacher and friends, and close liaison can help a school maintain a sense of continuity in periods of family breakdown or separation.

The role of the Education Welfare Officer came under scrutiny in the early 1970's. So many of their functions overlapped with social workers and a few local authorities dispensed with them. In retrospect, however, it seemed (Craft et al: 1978) that social workers were not as effective in curbing truancy. The calibre of EWOs varies considerably and their role as a link between home and school is an ambiguous one. Even in quite complex truancy problems, committed teachers who know the kind of difficulties children have in school might be more effective at persuading children to come and stay. Joanne came into the author's school half way through the third year and the indication from her previous school was that she hated it, ran out of lessons frequently and often stayed at home with her father's connivance. The EWO had a long waiting list and it was often 9.30 a.m. before he had finished his urgent telephone calls. Visits, threats and conversations with her step-father merely 'dramatized the evil' but so long as the visits were logged, the EWO was seen to be doing as much as the job required. The befriender, on the other hand, was told that Joanne was absent and by 9.05 a.m. she was on her way to the child's house. The excuse may have been that Joanne had forgotten to do her homework or she had overslept or she had to have a hated teacher first lesson. Tactfully, the befriender helped with the homework, waited quietly or negotiated with the about the teacher. Continuity of attendance was kept up, even at the cost of disciplinary flexibility. The child got a late mark rather than absence and she knew that there was someone in school who cared about her being there every day.

This kind of operation can only be mounted in exceptional cases. Day to day attendance rates are to some extend a function of local socio-economic conditions although they may well be influenced by punctilious checking across a range of tutorial staff. The co-ordinator should want to keep a watch on the attendance of slow learners and troublesome children, in common with other form tutors and senior members of the pastoral staff. Large scale truancy creates its own vicious circle of alienation and demoralization, which can only add to the problems of continuity in special educational provision. It may well be that in these cases, staff concerned with special education in this enlarged sense may wish to make home visits on a regular basis. In this case, reliance on an EWO might inhibit home-school links.

In a critical view of organizational aspects of transfer to special school, the American management theorist, Willower (1970), argues that ordinary schools are themselves 'discreditable' in their dealings with low expectation pupils. They often have something to hide. The professionals who act as the 'gatekeepers' preserve this 'spoiled identity'. There is all too often a difference between what the experts say pupils are like and what the pupils perceive. Casting the psychologists and social workers in the role of experts in the children's needs creates a situation where the individual's needs are focused on rather than deficiencies within the school. The psychologists, social workers and EWOs may themselves be unaware of any such deficiencies because of their status as outsiders. Hence an official analysis of the child's needs by an outside agency may hide the needs of the school and of its disciplinary and curricular structure.

In situations where the school has played its part in the reinforcement of disruptive behaviour, or the fulfilment of low expectations, and where the befriender is in close contact with the individual and his parents, the position of the teacher can become extremely ambiguous. The role of the Co-ordinator of Special Education may be of use, especially when it implies an inside knowledge of his own school and the special schools nearby and an understanding of the outside agencies. The ethical situation envisaged by the original departmental inquiry of 1898, in which 'dull children' need to be protected from teachers who want to 'pass them through their hands', might be quite different when there is a body of staff determined on wider integration.

Chapter Seven

PARENTS

When the Warnock Committee referred to 'Parents as Partners' they seem to have been concerned with severely handicapped children. There was a feeling that professionals often acted as if they knew more than the parents about their children's needs. Professionals also underestimated what parents could do for their children's education. The great majority of children with 'Special Educational Needs' are in the ordinary schools, yet the Committee made few recommendations about professional relations with their parents. It could be argued that the same points could be made on their behalf. The fact that they were not may reflect the differing social backgrounds of the two groups. Severe disabilities are evenly socially distributed. Children with the lowest expectations in ordinary schools came from the lowest socio-economic classes predominantly. The Warnock Committee specifically excluded the causes of handicap from its terms of reference. In this way it avoided having to elucidate the relationship between social class, illiteracy and 'abnormal behaviour'. As a result it was hardly in a position to look at the complex issues of reshaping teacher expectations of parents.

There seems to be little doubt that illiteracy is a largely working class phenomenon. Even amongst manual workers the least skilled have the greatest chances of having children who cannot read very well. That is not to say the relationship between type of employment and children's reading is a causal one. A Scottish survey of reading standards by Maxwell (1977) found that 40 per cent of working class children have average reading scores or better. Nevertheless, a great many educational sociologists have examined the economic and cultural attributes of working class parents in order to explain this association. Joyce Morris (1966) found fewer books and fewer instances of parents reading to children in working class homes. This is of particular interest in the light of the primary school researched by the author (see page 24 above). The Headteacher had ensured that no children left his school with reading ages lower than ten. One of his strategies had been to send children home with books and expect their parents to hear them reading regularly. Other sociological studies have focused on the characteristics of working class speech (e.g. Bernstein: 1971; Tough: 1977) or working class conceptual structures (Deutsch and Deutsch: 1968). In an experiment which heralded the start of the American Headstart programme, Rick Heber (1977) selected a group of poor inner city black parents whose tested IQ was below 70 and involved their infants in an intensive programme of cognitive development and themselves in a maternal care course. As a result, none of the experimental group had IQs of below 85, whilst one third of the control group had scores of less than 70. The basic assumption seems to have been that there is a range of attitudinal and cognitive defects in the family systems of the poor and it is these which generate school failure. The experiment was marred by the large number of variables employed by the researchers. The mothers also had a vocational training programme and they were provided with creches and employment in relatively well paid jobs. If they lost their job they were given help in finding others. Changing economic status and attitude shifts that this brought might have been at least as responsible for changes in response to formal IQ tests as the cognitive programmes.

The idea that poor families, especially from ethnic minority groups, have genetic defects which affect their intelligence was revived at the first signs of the failure of Headstart (e.g. Jensen: 1972; Eysenck: 1973). Richard Herrnstein (1971) even argued that ghetto families should be treated to a kibbutz-like upbringing so that their children should receive appropriate preparation for school. It had long been argued by students of Negro speech that this was just as logical and flexible as standard English. An ethnographic study of the language of gang leaders in Detroit by Labov (1970) demonstrated that children who had failed in school were capable of rigorous and sustained logical argument. He suggested that non standard English dialects should be viewed as different rather than defective and that the major problem was political. Middle class children spoke and thought in standard English. Standard English had a monopoly in academic writing - like for example sociolinguistics. This made it unlikely that Negro dialect speakers would be able to construct a critique of standard English in academicably acceptable terms. And it also explained why intelligent dialect speakers so often failed in school.

The traditional approaches of Remedial Education lend support to the idea that there are innate defects in the parents of slow learning children. Cyril Burt saw these as temperamental as well as cognitive:

> If, however, I were to single out the one feature in the home which showed the closest relation to the child's school progress, it would be, not the economic or industrial status of the family, but the efficiency of the mother. We have already noted how closely this conditions the child's

> physical development during the first few years of life. But in later years it has an immediate influence no less profound on the child's whole intellectual growth. At the same time, by affecting his comfort, cheerfulness, conscientiousness and bodily fitness from day to day, it acts through subtler channels indirect and direct. Wherever the mother is lacking in intelligence or temperamental stability, or in general force of character, where she is indifferent to the mental welfare of her family or herself overburdened by domestic worries or by frailties of heredity or health, there the child's mental and moral development suffers together.

The ringing certainties of Burt's arguments somehow miss the point that 'maternal efficiency' might not be such a crucial issue in an affluent family. The personal attributes of the parents seem to Burt the cause of the child's difficulties. Theirs is the responsibility for poor relations between home and school:

> Sometimes the parents cannot or will not co-operate. Sometimes they are openly hostile. Antagonism between parent and teacher, between the home and the school authority is nearly always infectious and becomes a frequent cause of indifference or opposition in the child.

Such analysis, which assigns parental attitudes and home conditions a dominant role in home-school relations, has characterized much of the subsequent prescriptions of remedial education. Tansley and Gulliford (1960) see the investigation of home circumstances as a prerequisite of removal from ordinary school. The number of books in the house, domestic arrangements and the linguistic performance of the parents must all be taken into account.

If, however, we were to argue that part of the problem stems from differences rather than defects and that the low expectations of teachers exacerbate children's difficulties, the relation between teachers and parents appears quite differently. It has to be accepted that parents like Graham's do think that school is 'rubbish' and that the teachers' claims to be an authority ought to be resisted. However, it is equally true that where children are seen as stupid, where they cannot read, where they have overwhelming social problems or criminal convictions, few teachers can conceive of consulting their parents about their children's needs. The author found the following Headteacher's remarks typical of a large number of teachers, whether they considered themselves 'liberal' or 'traditional' (Sewell: 1981). Whilst it be 'nice to get such parents' opinions, the concept of 'partnership' would be abandoned in a crisis about educational provision:

I'm afraid that my opinion is that the vast majority of children who create problems in school will come from backgrounds which are uncaring - not necessarily in terms of violence or neglect, but uncaring in the sense of the child at school. You might have a problem and the parents will say, 'Take him and cane him!', as if that will solve everything. Or else there is the other attitude: at school he's your problem, at home he's mine - you solve it. I think that a lot of children who cause us anxieties in terms of behaviour come from that sort of background in the first place. I also think that a reasonable number of children with learning difficulties have parents who also have similar learning difficulties. I know it sounds like a hereditary argument, but for example the child who is five years behind in terms of reading has a father who can't read, or there's nothing to read in the house. Parents have never read to their children. This is the sort of problem. We feel that the sort of help we can expect from parents is probably very limited. In terms of the ultimate decision about what should happen to a child, I think while it would be nice to get a parent's opinion, in the end you get to the position in a severe crisis where the parental wishes are overridden.

The author's research into Transfer to Special Schools (Sewell: 1981) also showed that whilst there are a few psychologists who would welcome parents to Case Conferences, articulate parents who speak the same language as the professionals are often preferred. Whilst this probably affects more working class parents of children with moderate learning difficulties, middle class parents can also be penalized, if their views do not coincide with those of the psychologist. Chazan et al (1970) provide an ironical example of five parents whose knowledge of the system enabled them to fight for their children:

Some of the parents were not realistic about their children's handicap and a few of them engaged in battles with the authorities to secure attendance in an ordinary school ... In all these cases, the placement worked out well.

In issues of transfer, it is difficult for parents not to feel the 'them and us' situation reported by Warnock. They feel they know their child as well as any professional and yet this knowledge is discounted. If only their co-operation was sought some of the 'special educational needs' might be alleviated. Such is the case in some of the Moscow and Leningrad schools visited by a UNESCO team (Segal: 1966). There would appear to be no special or remedial classes and once a child started in the ordinary school system, removal to a special school was virtually unknown. Slow learners were either labelled brain injured or 'oligophrenics' at the pre-school stage, or they were considered as normal. If, for any reason, they fell behind in their school work, the teacher first called on the parents' help. Devereux, who led the delegation which looked at how well the low attainers fared in ordinary schools, wrote:

> This does not mean that all pupils are equally able, but once a child is accepted, every attempt is made to keep him in the school and prevent his falling behind ... As soon as a child is seen to be finding the work difficult, there are discussions with the parents. They are always advised not to employ private coaches but they sometimes do. Instead they are offered extra lessons in groups of two, three or four for which teachers receive additional remuneration. This is part of the free educational service to students over seven years.

Whilst it can be argued that these Leningrad schools are showcases, that they represent the Soviet ideal rather than the common level and that reliable comparative information about the academic attainments of low achievement pupils was not made available to Segal's group, there is evidence from other sources of much closer parental involvement (Grant: 1970). The pressures that the State can bring to bear on parents to make them help with homework are considerable. In a social context where differences in wealth are much less, and where there is much greater State intervention in the running of schools, teacher expectations of working class parents might be much higher.

The power of individual teachers or Headteachers to gain similar co-operation in this country is constricted. However, in the case of the primary school mentioned earlier (see page 24 above) there were considerable attempts to involve them. Pupils were set reading and spelling homeworks from an early age. Letters were sent home outlining ways in which parents could help. Where parents were listening to their children's reading, this rekindled their own interests. The Headteacher quietly encouraged parents 'to hang onto the books after the children had finished'. One particular book, 'The Bonnie Pit Laddie' (Grice: 1970), was set in a neighbouring pit village. There were local Durham landmarks and many of the incidents had analogies in their own experiences. Some of the parents particularly enjoyed reading this and the Headteacher had run through several copies. There was no PTA as such. The parents came to the school regularly to discuss their children's progress and they sometimes chatted with the Headteacher about common interests.

The ethical problems involved in special education teachers making contact with older pupils' parents are more complex, however. Some schools have specific open evenings where parents of low attainers are invited to discuss progress and where the mechanics of reading teaching are explained. This gets round the difficulty that when general parents' evenings are held, the parents of low expectation pupils are wary of coming. Some expect to be criticized for their children's difficulties, or fear the chagrin of being told in front of a queue of more successful children's parents that their children are failures. Even these special education evenings make their children's status public and parents feel ambivalent about meeting anyone else they know.

Where individual home visits are considered, the pupils' own wishes have to be taken into account. There may be little point if the child distrusts his teacher or hates reading. If the parents back the teacher up, the child's dislike may be exacerbated. The child may not want the extent of his problem made clear to his parents. The child may know of a parent's illiteracy and feel that a conversation with the teacher might be received as a threat. A great deal may be accomplished even where the child thinks his parents don't care or can't read. The parents' willingness is crucial. It is as easy to teach parents to teach reading as it is teachers, and the results can be even better (Hewison and Tizard: 1980).

A child called Betty has undiagnosed hearing loss and her despair about school had led to chronic truancy. She was referred to a unit for disruptive pupils and although her reading had stuck at a reading age of eight and a half, her attitudes had changed. Her mother had had a number of long term emotional problems and an older brother was notoriously difficult. Three half hour visits, which included reading teaching demonstrations with the child, ensured that her mother listened to Betty read for half an hour every night for six nights a week. With complimentary help in school and at the unit, Betty made more than a year's progress in a term. It was no longer necessary for anyone to hear her now that she was more accurate and fluent. It only needed her mother to insist that she read herself half an hour every night before going to sleep to maintain progress. The realization that someone who knew her mother was also keeping a close eye on attendance also stopped the truancy.

In another case also involving a pupil with hearing loss, it was proving impossible for James to progress past a reading age of eight. The problems were more technically complex. His sight vocabulary sustained him up to that point, but his inability to analyse sounds or diversify his knowledge of phoneme/grapheme combinations made him gabble his way through unfamiliar words. James was too frightened about the possibility that people might know how deaf he was that he resisted any attempts to clarify his oral reading. He was also loath to comment on what he had read, and his comprehension was not developing. The junior school records showed that his mother was always helpful, while an early psychologist's report hinted at a fear of strangers. When his mother was told that what he needed was practice in breaking down long words and in talking about what the story was about, she agreed to help. She was warned that her son's refusal to co-operate with the reading staff probably hid quite a lot of anger. In the first two weeks, he was extremely truculent but his trust in his own family was that much greater than his trust in the teacher. The mother knew the child that much better and could get round his bad moods. This enabled her to be a much more effective reading teacher and after a month or so, James's reading began to improve. In this case, much of the diagnostic work had been done in advance by the teacher and the parent was given the benefit of his advice. As long as she knew what the teacher wanted her to do, she could carry out the teaching in her own way.

It may be that in the role of befriender, staff may be asked by a pupil to talk to his parents. Except in such circumstances it is difficult to maintain the child's confidence. The relationship of teacher to parent can hardly be a dogmatic one. Just as the teacher has reflected the child's values and thoughts back to him, he must now listen in much the same non-directive and uncritical way to his parents. It may well be that from the pupil's perspective, it seems the parents wish to deny any role in the child's difficulties. In one session the parents of a boy called Brian discussed with the author their efforts with their son, their sense of success, their elder daughter's problems - anything but what the boy felt to be their sense of disappointment in him. Eventually, just as the cups of tea have been drunk and the hour was drawing to a close, Brian's father said: 'Brian is like a pet dog. In the evenings I take him out for walks by the reservoir and he runs about all over the place, having the time of his life.' It was only necessary to reflect back to the father that playing with Brian was easier and more fun than treating him more as a normal fourteen year old, for the father to realize the difference between his own concept of the relationship and what actually existed. Previously when the parents had been called to the school to discuss Brian's bad school report, they had refused to accept any responsibility. A shouting match between the father and the pastoral tutor had ensued. In their own home and after a long non-judgemental discussion, the parents could accept feelings that would otherwise have remained hidden.

In some schools, special teachers make more than thirty visits a year, getting to know the area well, meeting parents in pubs as well as homes. There is always a degree of risk. The most obvious, although the most rarely encountered, is physical. Parents feel they have got a right to get angry in their own homes and professional status is little defence to a teacher then. One colleague of the author's even had her knee stroked on one visit. In practice, however, the greater risk is that the teacher finds he has started something that he is not personally or professionally equipped to finish. The visit could start with a discussion of a child's academic difficulties and then the parents might turn the conversation to their own marital difficulties, for instance. One boy called Ted resented his not having much pocket money and felt his mother was always irritated with him. On the visit of the author's the mother was just finishing a pile of ironing and her own clothes were old and threadbare. Her husband had cut off her maintenance and she was at her wit's end. She knew what a bad time her son was having at school and she knew she did not make life any easier for him. But she found it difficult enough to cope with her own anxieties, let alone his.

Not all visits will be as demanding as these and it may well help to time them so that there is good news to take home. A pupil is doing particularly well in reading or he has learned to control his temper. The parents may be asked what they think of his schooling, how it could be improved. One colleague had worked particularly effectively with a partially sighted pupil called Richard. A visit was arranged and the parents explained that although they were grateful for her efforts, there was only one other teacher who appeared to be 'bothered'. Their son had come home upset because he could not read the blackboard or because the ink on the worksheets was indistinct. Richard felt he could get away with any misbehaviour because all the teachers felt sorry for him. His mother was taking an Open University degree, despite her own partial sightedness and she had had great hopes of this boy. She had told the school he needed to be helped but that he also needed to be pushed, but no-one had done anything.

In this sense, talking to parents is a two-way affair, each side modifying its views of the other. In the overwhelming majority of cases the risks involved are imaginary rather than real. Such contacts create a fund of goodwill for the school and heighten parental expectations of their children's education. As such, they perform an important function in the reshaping of remedial education.

Chapter Eight

NEEDS, RIGHTS AND OBLIGATIONS

The concept of 'special educational needs' was warmly received when the Warnock Report was published. It seemed to offer a bridge between handicapped children and the non-handicapped. For those who deviated most from the norm in ordinary schools, it seemed to promise a better thought out and more individualized provision. It also suggested that there were common goals in the education of able, average and poor attaining pupils. Following Lewis and Vulliamy's article (1980) on 'The Sorcery of Definitions', however, it has received considerable criticism. It has been argued that the Warnock Committee placed too much emphasis on the learner and the special provision and not enough on the ordinary day to day interactions of teachers and pupils. The research on the effectiveness of previous special and remedial provision has not been encouraging. It has even been suggested that the expansion of special provision might be of rather more benefit to those concerned with the smooth running of the educational system than to the children by whom it was supposedly needed.

Social psychology has contributed greatly to our understanding of the way society tries to 'help' its deviants. This approach depends on our acceptance of the idea that we all develop a concept of ourselves through our interaction with others. This grows as we respond to society and it shapes our further interaction. So, the realization that we have visual difficulties affects our sense of identity. This sense of identity may be as crucial for our school learning as the visual difficulties themselves. It affects what we think we are capable of and how we shall deal with the world. The Warnock Report chose to focus on the educational implications of handicap rather than its causes. Yet the inter-relation of formal learning and learning about identity was also left unconsidered. To have examined it might well have cast doubts on the concept of 'special educational needs'.

One of the earliest books to have differentiated between deviations from social norms and the effects of this on the self concept was Edwin Lemert's 'Human Deviance: Social Problems and Social Control' (1967). This complex and original work argued that the social function of deviance imputation was societal solidarity. Defining an individual as deviant helped the majority in any society define itself as normal. Not all of those who fulfil legal and medical definitions of deviance are so imputed. Responses to incidents of deviance range from deviance imputation to concealment, tolerance and normalization. However, the act of being defined as deviant was potentially destructive to the individual. Where it entailed being treated as a child or as sick, it could lead to what Lemert referred to as 'secondary deviation'.

Since then, writers like Jaehnig (1975) and Fraser (1980) have developed the concept of the 'handicapped identity'. They distinguish between disability, which is part of the individual, and handicap, which relates to the physical and social environment. Their ideas can be illustrated by reference to Richard, the partially sighted pupil described at the end of the previous chapter. Richard suffered from a series of visual problems which included long sight, astigmatism and nystagmus. Nystagmus is a hereditary condition which shows itself in rapid involuntary movements of the eyeball. Richard's maternal grandfather also suffered in this way. He had overcome his difficulties to such an extent that he had had a job as a chef. Tremendous pressure was put on the family throughout Richard's school life for him to be sent to a residential school for the partially sighted, but the mother withstood this. At first Richard went to an ordinary infants school. Theteachers objected that the school was not adapted for a visually impaired child. There were stairs to contend with, the playground was bumpy and the toilets could only be reached by crossing it. There were no special aids in terms of lighting and magnifiers and none of the staff had training in special education. After two years the family moved to a town where there was a unit for partially sighted children and in the small groups provided, Richard learned to read Braille and, later, ink print. Ink print was in fact easier for him to master and his reading age went up to just over seven. His conservation was still poor and because of poor left/right co-ordination he often wrote 2 for 5, 6 for 9 and confused addition and multiplication signs. His handwriting and spelling were still very poor but Richard had made a start, mainly in his words, because the teacher was bothered about children like him.

The family moved again and Richard was put in the progress class of a secondary modern school. The teachers found him difficult to cope with. He was cantankerous, lazy and extremely difficult to keep occupied. With slow learners they could always find some sort of written exercise to keep them busy and if that failed they would give them drawing. Richard's eyesight made them unsure of what he could do and unwilling to punish him for misbehaviour. As many writers on visual impairment have brought out (e.g. Davis: 1963), blindness in others makes many people overprotective, fearful and embarrassed. After renewed pressure to persuade Richard's parents to accept special school placement, he moved to his fourth school. The same problems developed and Richard did little work. Eventually he was given individual attention in reading and in History. The History teacher was convinced that despite his disability and reading and writing difficulties, Richard was a talented historian. She arranged for the CSE examination to be put on tape and for Richard to record his answers orally. After a great deal of extra attention, at lunchtimes and after school, Richard passed at Grade One. He was then persuaded to go to an FE college for the visually impaired. The course he was on had three main aspects - basket weaving, braille and mobility training. Richard had no wish to learn canework, he could already read ink print and despite all the hazards, he successfully negotiated the public transport system of the area without any help. Richard developed what he called 'a real chip' after that special educational provision. He was out of work for a year afterwards because he felt that the world owed anyone as disabled as himself a living.

According to Fraser's theory, handicap is divided into a range of factors which themselves cover the medical, environmental and social psychological perspectives. Handicapping factors 'A' relate to the disability itself - sensory impairment, physical disability, etc. In Richard's case they can be represented by his visual difficulties. Handicapping factors 'B' relate to those aspects of the physical environment that make life difficult for the disabled. An example of this could be the stairs, playground and lighting of Richard's first infant school. Handicapping factors 'C' are those aspects of social interaction which bring about the handicapped identity. Through Richard's interaction with teachers in ordinary schools and college, he had mastered the art of getting out of work. He had developed 'abnormal behaviour': truancy, hoax calls to the Fire Brigade and so on. He felt abnormal and resentful. Both sectors of the educational system had played their part in amplifying his difficulties even though individual teachers from both sectors had shown how much could be done to minimise his handicaps.

The Warnock Committee would argue that Richard 'needed' extra reading attention, magnifiers, lighting, tape recorders, small groups and so on. Yet the case study illustrates one of the difficulties with special educational needs as a concept. Just because he was visually impaired it was assumed he would benefit from all these, as well as braille, canework and mobility training. By definition these would be considered special educational provision. Far from helping Richard, the last three further alienated him. Hence special education can not be defined only in terms of provision and disability. It must also be seen in terms of its effects on the sense of identity. What actually helps one pupil may harm another.

If we analyse Fraser's theory in terms of the children in the care of our ESN(M) schools and remedial classes, it could be argued that most of them have no handicapping factor 'A'. It is true that many have minor visual, hearing and constitutional problems but as the evidence of Burt (1937),

Morris (1966) and Clark (1971) would indicate, so do just as many academically successful children. Most of these children appeared normal to their parents and friends before they went to school. Many of them lead unexceptional lives after they leave. Edgerton (1969) suggests that unemployment, divorce and conviction rates are no higher among these young adults than among their peers from similar socio-economic backgrounds. In other words, it is only for the duration of school that many of them are handicapped. Hence the paradox; despite all the advances in medicine and psychology, our society handicaps a higher proportion of its young than any other and it does so through schools.

As an earlier essay of Mary Warnock's points out (Warnock: 1975), the fact that everyone in our society has to go to school affects our notions of equality. As a result we talk not only of a child's 'right' to education, but of his parents' 'obligations' to send him and his own 'need' to receive the goods that schools provide. The most obvious of these needs are the most basic. Children who fail to grasp the three Rs are handicapped in a society where minimal standards of literacy and numeracy are expected. In a society which has no such minimal expectation, the illiterate can survive a lot more easily. If the children who are traditionally the concern of remedial departments lived in pre-industrialized Britain or some parts of the Third World, they would not have appeared abnormal. Classroom failure or a late start in reading are for our society what anthropologists would call 'culturally visible events'. So it could be argued that the existence of universal education itself handicaps some children. If someone became visually handicapped as a result of his day to day contact with schools, the individual would have the right of compensation. Similarly, if through his day to day interaction with school a child became progressively more handicapped in intellectual or behavioural terms, he also ought to be entitled to a form of compensation. It is not enough, in terms of natural justice, to talk of the child's needs. One must also talk of the school's obligations.

In Mary Warnock's article on the Concept of Equality in Education (Warnock: op cit), she argues that there should be an unequal distribution of resources to enable backward readers to survive. She adopts the analogy of the division of a cake. In a situation where no special rights are involved, the cake ought to be equally divided. However, in many instances there will be an agreement about special rights. These rights would allow quantitatively unequal shares to be regarded as just. Where people are acknowledged to be unequal, as in the range of abilities, some ought to be permitted extra if this will help them to survive:

> Now in the case of the useful skills, such as swimming or indeed reading and writing, it is sensible to argue that everyone ought to have at least the bare minimum of skill (to enable

> them, for instance, to keep afloat if they fall into the river) even if it takes more time and resources to teach some people than to teach others.

Such an issue is straightforward enough in terms of the three Rs but the blandness of Warnock's argument becomes more obvious when she considers the broader curriculum. In order to provide children who have difficulties with the basic skills with a liberal education, their special rights would have to be extended. At this point she suggests philosophical arguments about equality and justice are often drowned in political disputes, and rather than enter them herself, she frames the issues as questions:

> Moreover the objection that for some people it is going to be far more difficult than others to reach a comparable minimum standard in cultural-heritage-appreciation or independent thought, takes on a new dimension. Does the equal right to an education entail that the naturally disadvantaged should have more education than those to whom it comes more easily?

It could be argued that if the context of failure deprives the most deviant of a chance of a liberal education, they have rights, in terms of natural justice, to some form of compensation. To return to Fraser's theoretical framework, the evidence would be that once children are 'disadvantaged', handicapping factors 'C' often accumulate. 'Inappropriate teaching' and teaching which 'simply responds to (without enhancing) lows' present motivational and ability levels' constitutes the bulk of their experience, according to Brophy and Good (1974). Richard's 'natural disadvantages' in terms of his hereditary visual impairments were less significant when it came to finding a job than the secondary deviation he had undergone during schooling. Sam and Malcolm and most of the other children mentioned in this book had no such 'natural disadvantages'. Their difficulties were compounded by the school system.

Dearden points out that statements of needs can be rather too flexible to be of much use philosophically (Dearden: 1972). Motives can colour needs statements:

> They may be used, for example, to explain, concede, recommend, justify, warn, advise, exhort and so on.

Psychologists often use statements of need and think that in doing so they avoid value judgements. Motivation can be ascribed to the reduction of need: 'The man ate because he was hungry. He felt the need for food.' Yet Dearden would argue that there are social and ethical elements to statements even as simple as these. A Westerner's sense of need might be quite different from an Indian's, and a Western psychologist's assumptions about the need for food would immediately become clear in a different cultural context. Dearden argues that ethical consensus is an important prerequisite in psychological assessments of need:

> When there is consensus on the ethical question, however, it is the scientist who has the important point to make; but where the normative assumptions significantly differ, needs statements may be culture based.

Dearden's caveats are so well known in philosophical circles that the role of 'special educational needs' in a report written under Mary Warnock's chairmanship is all the more puzzling. The remedial teacher, threatened with the closure of his department in order to help examination classes thrive, will be all too aware of the ambiguities of needs statements. Insofar as every pupil is an individual, each has special educational needs, arguably. It could be usggested that the Oxford University philosophy undergraduate with his expectation of a place in upper echelons of the Civil Service has a special educational need for his small group seminars. Many school teachers would argue that the needs of the most able children were more special than those of backward readers. Society can expect a greater return on its investment in the first than the second, and so can the pupils concerned. In order to confront such issues, the remedial teacher is forced to drop needs statements and return to more fundamental concepts like social justice and social obligations. He is also likely to make statements about the political implications of educational failure. Statements about the case for providing children with the bare minimum of skills, 'even if it takes more time and resources to teach some people than others' are political, even though Mary Warnock would disagree:

> Notoriously, political theorists concerned with education have to try to devise further arguments to justify this policy or that in their distribution of resources. All I hope to have suggested is that no appeal to equality will on its own help to make good decisions in this field.

The major practical difficulty with the Warnock Committee's proposals is that they ignore the effects of stigma and handicapping factors 'C'. They promise little in the over-turning of low expectations among failing pupils. The evaluative evidence of remedial education is that it offers many children short term benefits, but that a few are harmed and that it makes little difference in the long term. It would appear from the evidence outlined in Chapter Two that the pedagogical strategies and the educational knowledge of the remedial teachers matter less in the long term than their interpersonal skills and their ability to help low expectation pupils in the broader curriculum. In this respect, the Co-ordinator of Special Education is directly involved in ethical decisions about the distribution of personnel. Which children are taught to read by which teachers might constitute a more reliable guarantee of their right to that basic skill than the setting up of a resource room per se.

The further one moves from a skills curriculum towards a liberal education, the more difficult it becomes to make statements about rights, as Mary Warnock's earlier article on equality also makes clear. In following the American path towards an objectives approach to the curriculum, and recommending regular evaluations of individual progress involving parents and teachers, the Warnock Committee may well have felt they had found a solution. Yet the White Paper that followed the Report suggested that regular parent/teacher reviews would be too difficult to arrange in every ordinary school and that it must be left to the Headteacher's discretion. There is little evidence that an objectives approach to the curriculum produces consistent or long term benefits for low expectation pupils, especially where it lacks judicial support and mandatory parental inspection. Asking Heads of departments to produce curricula for slow learners might be less effective than informal liaison with subject teachers who have already been shown to work well with backward readers.

Needs statements are unlikely to gain credibility as the recession deepens. It is painfully ironic that the Wood Committee's recommendations about special classes in ordinary schools came at the beginning of the last great depression (H.M.S.O.: 1929). Government supported recommendations made little practical impression then, and it may be that people are wary of undertaking new risks at times of financial contraction. The handicap of illiteracy is not lessened in times of recession, of course. There is little indication that poor readers necessarily make poor employees in times of prosperity, but when competition for jobs is greater, illiteracy, like membership of ethnic minority groups, becomes an even greater stigma. Hence the obligation on schools to teach children to read and extend their wider educational provision must be re-affirmed.

It has been argued throughout the book that statements of special educational need could be used as a cover for the needs of the teachers, Headteachers and other professionals. In practical terms, it may be in the interests of the partially sighted pupil who can read to spend as little time as possible in the company of sighted pupils who can not. A resource room which was used as a 'sanctuary' for difficult pupils might do little to help the poor readers in it, either. In that part of the curriculum not concerned with the teaching of basic skills, it is the co-ordinator's responsibility to secure the widest and the most challenging teaching possible, whether or not this is done by special class staff or based on written curricular objectives. It may well be useful for the co-ordinator to use Brennan's model of curriculum development as a basis for negotiation with subject departments. But the grounds of his professional claims are that there is a minority of teachers who 'reach out forcefully and successfully to involve low achievers' (Brophy and Good: 1974), who can be used firstly to teach reading and secondly to reinforce the effective teaching of these low achievers in their departments. Hence instead of proliferating resource room staff who might be especially vulnerable in times of recession, the co-ordinator uses the human resources of his school to provide an informal group of effective subject specialist teachers. Some contribute to language across the curriculum, others act as 'named teachers' within their departments and others work as a support group.

Closer co-operation between lower school curriculum groups might make special classes redundant there and, given an effective support group, it may be possible to disperse the 'non exam' group. Members of this minority group would liaise closely with external agencies like SPS, Social Services and EWOs. In the possibility, mentioned in Chapter Six, that these agencies were caught in the role of social control and that this did not represent the children's interests, the support group would be prepared to take the dominant role. Criteria for success would be a vital concern to the co-ordinator in all aspects of the curriculum and in issues of support and control. As well as quantitative data such as reading scores and delinquency rates, pupils', ex-pupils' and parents' views would play an important role in continuing reviews.

As a corollary to a co-ordinated special educational policy within the school, co-ordinators and other teachers from a range of schools could get together to form Warnock Action Research Groups. From the indications of the Warnock Report itself, it appears as if in-service work would be envisaged as a lecture/workshop course on such apparently unproblematic topics as incidence, assessment and prescriptive teaching. Our definitions of special education incorporate a critique of present educational provision. One way to get teachers to improve the situation for low attainers is to think out goals and methods for themselves. Teachers involved in such groups would have to be as hard-headed as they were tender-hearted. These Warnock Action Research Groups would act as discussion groups where actual provision is analysed and argued over. Especially interesting and practicable curriculum projects could be taken back to other schools and used to put pressure on other subject departmental Heads and the Headteacher.

Where even this produced little shift in attitudes, advisors and inspectors might be informally invited into the school. An afternoon's visit may have little long term effect so they could perhaps come and work a week. An intensive school based in-service course could be mounted, based on the actual school setting and proposals for curriculum development, tailored to the actual teachers' capabilities. Where the low status of the co-ordinator itself seems to be inhibiting change, the advisor could recommend larger in-service training for him.

Such a role is already being carried out in some parts of the country and in these schools there may be a more accommodating attitude towards pupils from special schools, units and community homes. No doubt the demands of such a role would intimidate other Heads of remedial. For these, one might envisage a kind of rolling programme. At first all that is planned is to involve a few more staff in reading teaching and to get a County Advisor or a psychologist to arrange the training sessions. Later, curriculum development begins with a named teacher appointed to one department. Lastly, the support group begins to emerge. Now the co-ordinator may feel ready to dismantle the special class, confident that special education means something different from reading teaching and an integrated studies course for a small group of alienated fifth years.

Remedial education started in the 1920s as a response to the pressures on Board School teachers. Similar pressures still exist. There will always be teachers who want to 'pass all the dull children through their hands' (H.M.S.O.: 1898 op cit) and tender-hearted remedial staff willing to look after them. But, reshaped, remedial education could yet produce a fairer and more incorporative ethos in schools. The demands on the co-ordinator would be immense. Not only would he have to know enough about reading to show other adults how to teach it, but he must be enough of a polymath to interest colleagues in curriculum development in areas other than his own. He must have persistence and warmth. He must have an historical awareness of the fate of low status working class children and use this as the basis of his critique of present conditions.

BIBLIOGRAPHY

Ablewhite R.C., The Slow Reader: A Problem in Two Parts (Heinemann: 1967)

Ablewhite R.C., Mathematics and the Less Able (Heinemann: 1969)

Agard J.A., The Classroom Ecological Structure: quoted in Evaluating Mainstreaming Programmes: Models, Caveats, Considerations and Guidelines (Exceptional Children: 44: 588-601: 1978)

Ainscow M. and Tweddle D.A., Preventing Classroom Failure: An Objectives Approach (Wiley: Chichester: 1979)

Arbuckle D.S. Ed., Counselling and Psychotherapy: An Overview (McGraw: New York: 1967)

Ayllon T. and Azrin N., The Token Economy: A Motivational System for Therapy and Rehabilitation (Appleton Century Crofts: New York: 1968)

Barnes D., Britton J. and Rosen H., Language, the Learner and the School (Penguin: Harmondsworth: 1971)

Barton L. and Tomlinson S. Eds., Special Education: Policy Practices and Social Issues (Harper and Row: 1982)

Beck J. et al, Worlds Apart: Readings for a Sociology of Education (Collier MacMillan: 1976)

Becker H.S. Ed., The Other Side: Perspectives on Deviancy (Free Press: New York: 1964)

Becker W.C., Teaching Reading and Language to the Disadvantaged (Harvard Ed. Review 47: 4: 1977)

Behan B., Borstal Boy (Hutchinson: 1958)

Berne E., Games People Play (Ballantine: 1978)

Bernstein B., Class, Codes and Control, Vol. 1 (Routledge and Kegan Paul: 1971)

Binet A. and Simon T., Mentally Defective Children (Trans. Drummond W.B., Arnold: 1914)

Bransford J.D., Human Cognition: Learning, Understanding and Remembering (Wadsworth Pub. Co.: Belmont (Ca.): 1979)

Brennan W.K., Curricular Needs of Slow Learners: Report of the Schools Council Curricular Needs of Slow Learning Pupils Project (Evans Methuen Educational: Working Papers: No. 63: 1979)

Brophy J.E. and Good T.L., Teacher Student Relationships: Causes and Consequences (Holt: New York: 1974)
Burt C.L., Handbook of Tests for Use in Schools (King: 1923)
Burt C.L., The Backward Child (U.L.P.: 1937)
Carkhuff R.R. and Berenson B.G., Beyond Counselling and Therapy (2nd Ed., Holt: Rinehart Winston: 1977)
Carrington B. and Wood E.R., Race, Schooling and Sport: Paper presented to B.S.A. (Physical Education) Conference 1981 (to be published)
Cashdan A., Pumfrey P.D. and Lunzer E.A., Children Receiving Remedial Treatment in Reading (Educ. Res.: 13, 2, 98-105: 1971)
Chaffin J.D., Spellman C.R., Regan C.E. and Davison R., Two Follow-up Studies of Former Educable Mentally Retarded Students from the Kansas Work-Study Project (Exceptional Children: 37: 733-738: 1971)
Chazan M. et al, Some of our Children: the early Education of Children with Special Needs (Open Books: Shepton Mallet: 1980)
Chomsky C., Reading Writing and Phonology (Harvard Ed. Review 40: 287-309: 1971)
Cicourel A.V., Language Use and School Performance (Academic Press: New York: 1974)
Clark M.M., Reading Difficulties in Schools: A Community Study of Specific Reading Difficulties (Penguin: Harmondsworth: 1970)
Clay M.M., Reading: The Patterning of Complex Behaviour (2nd Ed.: Heinemann Educational: 1979)
Coard B., How the West Indian Child is made Educationally Subnormal in the British School System: The Scandal of the Black Child in Schools in Britain (New Beacon Books for Caribbean Education and Community Workers' Association: 1971)
Coleridge S.T., The Rime of the Ancient Mariner: in the Oxford Book of English Verse: Quiller-Couch, Sir A. (Clarendon Press: Oxford: 1900)
Collins J.E., The Effects of Remedial Education: Birmingham University Institute of Education Educational Monographs: No. 4 (Oliver and Boyd: Edinburgh: 1961)
Collins J.E., The Remedial Reading Hoax (Remedial Education: 7: 3: 9-10: 1972)
Coltham J.B. and Fines J., Educational Objectives for the Study of History: a Suggested Framework: Teaching of History Pamphlet No. 35 (Historical Association: 1971)
Cope C. and Anderson E., Special Units in Ordinary Schools: an Exploratory Study of Special Provision for Disabled Children (London University Institute of Education: 1977)
Cotterell G., Check List of Basic Sounds: Learning Development Aids (Wisbech: Cambs.: 1969)
Craft M., Raynor J. and Cohen L., Linking Home and School: a new review (3rd Ed.: Harper: 1980)

Curr W. and Gourlay N., An Experimental Evaluation of Remedial Education (Brit. J. Educ. Psychol. 23: 45-55: 1953)
Daniels J.C. and Diack H., The Standard Reading Tests (Chatto: 1958)
Davies G.W., The Attainments of Low Achieving School Leavers (Unpublished M.Ed Dissertation: Birmingham University: 1981)
Davis F., Deviance Disavowal: The Management of Strained Interaction by the Visibly Handicapped: in The Other Side: Becker H.S. Ed. (Free Press: New York: 1964)
Dearden R.F., Needs in Education: in Education and the Development of Reason: Dearden R.F., Hirst P.H. and Peters R.S. (Routledge and Kegan Paul: 1972)
Deutsch C. and Deutsch M., Theory of Early Childhood Environmental Programs: in Hess R. and Bear R. Eds.: Early Education: Current Theory, Research and Action (Aldine: Chicago: 1968)
Devereux K.F., The Education of Children in Ordinary Schools: in Backward Children in the U.S.S.R.: Segal S.S. (Arnold: Leeds: 1966)
Dewdney J.C. and Rhind D.W., People in Durham - a Census Atlas (Census Research Unit: Dept. of Geography: University of Durham: 1975)
Dexter L.A., On the Politics and Sociology of Stupidity in our Society: in The Other Side: Becker H.S. Ed. (Free Press: New York: 1964)
Dolan T., Dolan E., Taylor V., Shoreland J. and Harrison C., Improving Reading through Group Discussion Activities: in The Effective Use of Reading: Lunzer E.A. and Gardner K. (Heinemann Educational Books for the Schools Council: 1979)
Douglas J.W.B. et al, All Our Future: a Longitudinal Study of Secondary Education (Davies: 1968)
Dumont R.V. Jr. and Wax M.L., Cherokee School Society and the Intercultural Classroom (Human Organization: 28 (3) 217-226: 1969)
Duncan A., Teaching Mathematics to Slow Learners (Ward Lock: 1978)
Dunn L.M. Ed., Exceptional Children in the Schools: Special Education in Transition (2nd Ed.: Holt: New York: 1973)
Edgerton R., The Cloak of Competence (Berkeley: University of California Press: 1967)
Eysenck H.J., The Effects of Psychotherapy: An Evaluation (Journal of Consulting Psychology: 16 (4): 319-327: 1952)
Eysenck H.J., The Inequality of Man (Temple Smith: 1973)
Fernald G.M., Remedial Techniques in Basic School Subjects (McGraw: New York: 1943)
Fischer J., Does Anything Work? (Journal of Social Service Research: 1 (3): 215-243: 1978)
Fischer J. et al, Relationship between Theoretical Orientation and Therapists' Empathy, Warmth and Genuineness (J. Counsel. Psychol. 22: 399-403: 1975)

Foster G., Ysseldyke J. and Reese J., "I wouldn't have seen it if I hadn't believed": Exceptional Children (63: 617-624: 1972)
Fraser B.C., The Meaning of Handicap in Children: Child Care: Health and Development (6: 2: 83-91: 1980)
Frith U. Ed., Cognitive Processes in Spelling (Academic Press: 1980)
Fry E., Fry's Readability Graph: Clarifications, Validity and Extension to Level 17 (Journal of Reading: 242-252: December, 1977)
Furlong V.A., Anarchy Goes to School: A Case Study of Pupils' Knowledge of their Teachers: in School Experience: Woods P. and Hammersley M. Eds. (Croom Helm: 1977)
Galletley I., How To Do Away With Yourself (Remedial Education: 11: 3: 149-151: 1976)
Gesell A. and Thompson H., Learning and Growth in Identical Twins (Psychol. Monogr. v6: 1-124: 1929)
Gickling F.R. and Theobald J.T., Mainstreaming: Affect or Effect (Journal of Special Education: 9: 317-328: 1975)
Gillham W.E.C. Ed., Reconstructing Educational Psychology (Croom Helm: 1978)
Gilling T.B. and Rucker C.N., Labels and Teacher Expectations: Exceptional Children (43: 464-465: 1977)
Goffman E., Stigma: Notes on the Management of Spoiled Identity (Prentice Hall Inc., Englewood Cliffs: N.J.: 1963)
Goldstein H., Moss J. and Jordan L.J., The Efficacy of Special Class Training in the Development of Mentally Retarded Children (University of Illinois: Urbana, Ill. 1965)
Goodman K.S., Behind the Eye: What Happens in Reading: in Reading: Process and Program (National Council of Teachers of English: Urbana, Ill. 1970)
Grant N., Soviet Education (Penguin: Harmondsworth: 4th Ed. 1979)
Greenwood W., Love on the Dole (Jonathan Cape: 1933)
Gregory R.P., Individual Referrals: How Naive are Educational Psychologists? (Bull Brit. Psych. Soc.: 33: 381-384: 1980)
Grice F., The Bonny Pit Laddie (Oxford University Press: 1960)
Halsey A.H., Heath A.F. and Ridge J.M., Origins and Destinations: Family, Class and Education in Modern Britain (Oxford University Press: 1980)
Hallam R., Piaget and the Teaching of History (Educ. Res. 11: 200-206: 1969)
Hamilton D., Jenkins D., King C., MacDonald B. and Parlett M., Eds., Beyond the Numbers Game (MacMillan Education: Basingstoke: Hants: 1977)
Hargreaves D.H., Social Relations in a Secondary School (Routledge: 1967)
Hargreaves D.H., Hester S.K. and Mellor F.J., Deviance in Classrooms (Routledge: 1975)

Heber F.R., Research in the Prevention of Socio Cultural Retardation through Early Intervention (International Union of Child Welfare: 1: Geneva: 1977)

Henry J., Docility, or Giving Teacher What She Wants (Journal of Social Issues: 2: 33-41: 1955)

Henry J., Essays on Education (Penguin: Harmondsworth: 1971)

Hieronymus A.N., Linquist E.F. and France N., Richmond Tests of Basic Skills (N.F.E.R., Nelson: Windsor, Berks: 1982)

H.M.S.O., Report of the Departmental Committee on Defective and Epileptic Children (Board of Education: 2 vols.: 1898)

H.M.S.O., Report of the Joint Departmental Committee on Mental Deficiency (Wood Report): (Board of Education and Board of Control: 3 vols.: 1929)

H.M.S.O., Half Our Future: Report of the Central Advisory Council for Education (Newsom Report): (Ministry of Education: 1963)

H.M.S.O., Progress in Reading 1948-1964 (Education Pamphlet No. 50: 1966)

H.M.S.O., Slow Learner in Secondary Schools (Department of Education and Science: 1971)

H.M.S.O., A Language for Life (Report of the Committee of Inquiry Appointed by the Secretary of State for Education and Science under the Chairmanship of Sir Alan Bullock: 1975)

H.M.S.O., Circular 2/75: Discovery of Children Requiring Special Education and the Assessment of their Needs (Department of Education and Science: 1975)

H.M.S.O., Special Educational Needs: Report of the Committee of Inquiry into the Education of Handicapped Children and Young People under the Chairmanship of Mrs. H.M. Warnock (Department of Education and Science: 1978)

H.M.S.O., West Indian Children in our Schools: Interim Report of the Committee of Inquiry into the Education of Children from Ethnic Minority Groups under the Chairmanship of A. Rampton (Cmnd 8273: 1981)

H.M.S.O., Education Act (Ch. 60: 1981)

Herndon J., How to Survive in Your Native Land (Bantam Edition: 1972)

Herrnstein R., IQ: quoted in: IQ Tests: Building Blocks for the New Class System: Chomsky N. (Ramparts: 11: 26-30: 1972)

Hewison J. and Tizard J., Parental Involvement and Reading Attainment (Br. J. Educ. Psychol.: 50: 209-215: 1980)

Hirst P.H., The Logic of the Curriculum (Journal of Curriculum Studies: 1: 142-158: 1969)

Hirst P.H., Liberal Education and the Nature of Knowledge: in Education and the Development of Reason: Dearden R.F., Hirst P.H. and Peters R.S. (Routledge and Kegan Paul: 1972)

Holt J.C., How Children Fail (Penguin: Harmondsworth: 1969)

Hornsby B. and Shear F., Alpha to Omega: the A-Z of Teaching Reading (Heinemann: 1975)
Hotopf N., Slips in of the Pen: in Cognitive Processes in Spelling: Frith U. Ed. (Academic Press: 1980)
Hudson L., Contrary Imaginations: a Psychological Study of the English Schoolboy (Methuen: 1966)
Hull J., Practical Points on Teaching History to Less Able Secondary Pupils (Teaching History: 28: 14-23: 1980)
Jackdaw Publications Ltd., (1970)
Jaehnig W., A Handicapped Identity Part II: in A Handicapped Identity: Boswell D., Jaehnig W. and Mittler P. Eds. (O.U.: p.251: 1975)
Jamieson M., Parlett H. and Pocklington K., Towards Integration: a study of Blind and Partially Sighted Children in Ordinary Schools (N.F.E.R., Windsor: 1977)
Jensen A.R., Genetics and Education (Methuen: 1972)
Jones E., A Resource Approach to Meeting Special Educational Needs in a Secondary School: in Special Education: Policy, Practices and Social Issues: Barton L. and Tomlinson S. Eds. (Harper and Row: 1982)
Jones N. and Jones E., Oxfordshire Looks Towards the Future (Special Education Forward Trends: 8: 2: 23-25: 1981)
Jones R.L., Gottlieb J., Guskin S. and Yoshida R.K., Evaluating Mainstreaming Programmes: Models, Caveats, Considerations and Guidelines (Excaptional Children: 44: 588-601: 1978)
Kamin L.J., The Science and Politics of IQ (John Wiley: New York: 1974)
Keddie N., Classroom Knowledge: in Knowledge and Control: New Directions For the Sociology of Knowledge: M.F.D. Young, Ed. (Collier MacMillan Ltd.: West Drayton: Middx: 1971)
Kilpatrick J. and Wirsup I., Eds., The Psychology of Mathematical Abilities in School Children (University of Chicago Press: 1976)
Kohl H., Reading: How To (Penguin: Harmondsworth: 1974)
Kolstoe O.P., Teaching Educable Retarded Children (Holt, Rinehart and Winston: New York: 2nd Ed.: 1976)
Labov W., The Logic of Nonstandard English: in Language in Education: s Source Book: Cashdan A. et al, Eds. (Routledge and Kegan Paul for the Open University: 1972)
Lawrence D., The Effects of Counselling on Reading (Educational Research: 13: 2: 119-124: 1971)
Lawrence D.H., The Rainbow (Methuen: 1915)
Lawton D., The End of the Secret Garden: A study in the Politics of the Curriculum: an Inaugural Lecture (University of London: Institute of Education: 1979)
Lemert M.L., Human Deviance, Social Problems and Social Control (Printice Hall Inc., Englewood Cliffs: New Jersey: 1967)
Lewis I. and Vulliamy G., 'Warnock or Warlock?': The Sorcery of Definitions: The Limitations of the Report on Special Education (Educ. Rev. Vol 32. No. 1: 1980)

Lloyd J.D., An Evaluation of DISTAR (B.Ed Dissertation, Sunderland Polytechnic: unpublished: 1978)
Lofland J., Deviance and Identity (Prentice Hall Inc., Englewood Cliffs: New Jersey: 1969)
Lunzer E.A. and Gardner K., Edg., The Effective Use of Reading (Heinemann, for the Schools Council: 1979)
Lunzer E.A. and Gardner K., Eds., Reading for Learning in the Secondary Schools (to be published by the Schools Council)
McLeod J., GAP Reading Comprehension Test (Heinemann: 1970)
Malmquist E., Factors Related to Reading Disability in the First Grade of the Elementary School (Alquist and Wiksell: 1958)
Maxwell J., Reading Progress from 8 to 15: a Survey of Attainment and Teaching Practices in Scotland (N.F.E.F.: Windsor: 1977)
Mercer J.R., Career Problems of Persons Labeled as Mentally Retarded: reprinted in Rubington E. and Weinberg M.S., Deviance the Interactionist Perspective (MacMillan: New York: 1973, 2nd Ed.)
Mercer J.R., Labelling the Mentally Retarded (University of California Press: Berkeley: 1973)
Midwinter E.C., Ed., Projections: an Educational Priority Area at Work (Ward Lock Educational: 1972)
Miles T.R., On Helping the Dyslexic Child (Methuen Educational Ltd.: 1970)
Monroe M., Children Who Cannot Read (University of Chicago Press: Chicago: 1932)
Morris J.M., Standards and Progress in Reading (N.F.E.R.: Slough: 1966)
Morris M., How to Prove that Comprehensive Schools have not Failed (The Times: 2/4/80)
Morrison A. and McIntyre D. Eds., The Social Psychology of Teaching (Penguin: Harmondsworth: 1972)
Morton J., The Logogen Model and Orthographic Structure: in Cognitive Processes in Spelling: Frith U. Ed. (Academic Press: 1980)
Murray W., Teaching Reading (Ladybird Books Ltd., Loughborough: 1969)
Nash R., Classrooms Observed: the Teachers' Perception and the Pupils' Performance (Routledge: 1975)
N.F.E.R.: Nelson., Educational Guidance and Assessment (N.F.E.R.: Nelson Publishing: Windsor, Berks: 1982)
Norrie E., Om Ordblindbed (Copenhagen: 1939)
Parker D.H., S.R.A. Reading Laboratory (Science Research Associates Inc.: Chicago: 1963)
Partington J.A. and Hinchliffe G., Some Aspects of Classroom Management (British Journal of Teacher Education: 5: 3: 231-242: 1979)
Patrick J., A Glasgow Gang Observed (Eyre Methuen: 1973)
Penrose L.S., The Biology of Mental Defect: 2nd Ed. (Sidgwick and Jackson: 1954)
Peters M.L., Spelling: Caught or Taught? (Routledge: 1967)

Philips C.J., Summerfield and After: the Training of Educational Psychologists (Bulletin of the British Psychological Society 24: 207-213: 1971)
Platt A., Child Savers: in Worlds Apart: Beck J. et al, Eds. (Collier MacMillan: 1976)
Plunckett S., Decomposition and All That Rot (Teacher of Mathematics: 1977)
Power M.J., Benn R.T. and Morris J.N., Delinquent Schools? (New Society: 19th October, 1967)
Reynolds D., When Pupils and Teachers Refuse a Truce: the Secondary School and the Creation of Delinquency: in Mungham G. and Person G. Eds. Working Class Youth Culture (Routledge and Kegan Paul: 1976)
Reynolds D., The Delinquent School: in The Process of Schooling: Hammersley M. and Woods P. Eds. (Routledge and Kegan Paul: 1977)
Richards I.A., Practical Criticism: a Study of Literary Judgement (Routledge and Kegan Paul: 1929)
Rist R.C., Student Social Class and Teachers' Expectations: The Self Fulfilling Prophecy: in Ghetto Education (Harvard Educational Review: 40: 411-450: 1970)
Rogers C.R., Client Centred Therapy (Houghton: Boston, Mass: Constable: London: 1951)
Rosenberg M., Society and the Adolescent Self Image (Princeton University Press: Princeton (NJ): 1965)
Rutter M., Tizard J. and Whitmore K., Education, Health and Behaviour (Longman: 1970)
Rutter M. et al, Fifteen Thousand Hours: Secondary Schools and Their Effects on Children (Open Books: 1979)
Salvia J., Clark E. and Ysseldyke J., Teacher Retention of Stereotypes of Exceptionality (Exceptional Childreb: V 40: 651-652: 1973)
Satz P. and Fletcher J.M., Early Screening Tests: some uses and abuses (Journal of Reading Disabilities: 12: (1): 56-59: 1979)
Schonell F.J. and Schonell F.E., Diagnostic and Attainment Testing (Oliver and Boyd: Edinburgh: 1950)
Schools' Council, The Practical Curriculum (Schools' Council Working Paper 70: Methuen Educational: 1981)
Sczypka C., DISTAR - An Evaluation (Unpublished B.Ed Dissertation: University of Durham: 1981)
Segal S.S., Ed., Backward Children in the U.S.S.R.: a Report of the Visit to Moscow in June, 1965 of a Delegation of the Guild of Teachers of Backward Children (Arnold: Leeds: 1966)
Sewell G.J.F., Transfer to Special Schools - A Sociological Critique (Unpublished M.Ed Dissertation: Birmingham University: 1980)
Sewell G.J.F., The Micro Sociology of Segregation: Case Studies in the Exclusion of Children with Special Needs from Ordinary Schools: in Special Education: Policy Practices and Social Issues: Barton L. and Tomlinson S. Eds. (Harper and Row: 1982)

Sharp R. and Green A., Education and Social Control: a study in Progressive Primary Education (Routledge: 1975)
Shepherd M., Oppenheim A.N. and Mitchell S., Childhood Behaviour and the Child Guidance Clinic: an Epidemiological Study (J. Child Psychol. Psychiat. 7: 39-52: 1966)
Shotel J.R., Iano R.P. and McGettigan J.F., Teacher Attitudes Associated with the Integration of Handicapped Children (Exceptional Children: 38: 677-683: 1972)
Shuard H. and Quadling D., Eds., Teacher of Mathematics: Some Aspects of Professional Life (Harper: 1980)
Summers A.A. and Woolf B.L., Do Schools Make a Difference (American Economic Review: 1972)
Stake R.E., The Countenance of Educational Evaluation: in Beyond the Numbers Game: Hamilton et al Eds. (MacMillan Educational: Basingstoke, Hants: 1977)
Start K.B. and Wells B.K., The Trend of Reading Standards (N.F.E.R., Slough: 1972)
Stauffer R.G., The Language Experience Approach to the Teaching of Reading (Harper: New York: 1970)
Stockdale W., Talk, Write and Spell: The Basil Blackwell Spelling Box (Basil Blackwell: Oxford: 1978)
Sunday Times, Hints on Pronunciation for Foreigners (T.S.W. - only initials of writer known: from a letter published in the London Sunday Times: Jan. 3rd, 1965)
Sutton C.R., Language and Communication in Science Lessons: in The Art of the Science Teacher: Sutton C.R. and Haysom J.T., Eds. (Science Teacher Education Project: McGraw Hill: 1979)
Sykes G.M. and Matza D., Techniques of Neutralization: A Theory of Delinquency (American Sociological Review: 22: 667-670: 1957)
Szasz T.S., Ideology and Insanity (Calder and Boyars: 1970)
Tannenbaum F., Crime and the Community (Columbia University Press: New York: 1938)
Tansley A.E., Sound Sense (Arnold: Leeds: 1975)
Tansley A.F. and Gulliford R., The Education of Slow Learning Children (Routledge and Kegan Paul: 1960)
Tansley P. and Panckhurst J., Children with Specific Learning Difficulties: A Critical Review of Research (N.F.E.R. Nelson: Windsor: 1981)
Times Educational Supplement, How the Cuts Bite - Official (pp 18-19: 20: 2: 81)
Tomlinson S., Educational Subnormality: A Study in Decision Making (Routledge and Kegan Paul: 1981)
Tough J., Talking and Learning: a Guide to Fostering Communication Skills in Nursery and Infant Schools (Ward Lock: Drake Educational Associates: 1977)
Truax C.B. and Carkhuff R.R., Towards Effective Counselling and Psychotherapy: Training and Practice (Aldine: Chicago: 1967)
Warnock H.M., The Concept of Equality in Education (Oxford Review of Education 1: 1: 3-8: 1975)

Watts A.F., The Holborn Vocabulary Test for Young Children (Harrap: 1949)
Wedell K. and Lindsay G.A., Early Identification Procedures: What Have We Learned? (15: 3: 130-135: 1980)
Werthman C., Delinquents in Schools: a Test for the Legitimacy of Authority (Berkeley Journal of Sociology: 8: 1: 39-60: 1963)
Westwood P.S., Remedial Teachers' Handbook (Oliver and Boyd: 1975)
Wheldall K. and Congreve S., The Attitudes of British Teachers towards Behaviour Modification (Educ. Rev. 32: 1: 53-65: 1980)
Wilcox B. and Eustace P.J., Tooling up for Curriculum Review (N.F.E.R., Windsor: 1980)
Willis P.E., Learning to Labour: How Working Class Kids Get Working Class Jobs (Saxon House: Farnborough, Hants: 1977)
Willower D., Special Education: Organization and Administration (Exceptional Children: 36: 591-4: 1970)
Winett R.A. and Winckler R.C., Current Behaviour Modification in the Classroom: Be Still, Be Quiet, Be Docile (Journal of Applied Behaviour Analysis: 5: 494-504: 1972)
Woods P., The Divided School (Routledge: 1979)
Woods P. and Hammersley M. Eds., School Experience: Explorations in the Sociology of Education (Croom Helm: 1977)
Young D., Group Reading Test (Hodder and Stoughton: 1969)
Young M.F.D. Ed., Knowledge and Control: New Directions for a Sociology of Knowledge (Collier MacMillan Ltd.: West Drayton, Middx.: 1971)
Zykova V., Essays in the Psychology of Mastering Elementary Geometric Knowledge: Moscow (Uchped giz 1955) quoted in The Psychology of Mathematical Abilities in Schoolchildren: Krutetskii V.A.: Trans. Teller J., Kilpatrick J. and Wirszup I. Eds. (University of Chicago Press: Chicago: 1976)

INDEX

Advisors	1, 120-121
Behaviour Modification	87-89, 95
Brennan	37, 47-49, 71, 78, 119
Brophy and Good	7-8, 18, 26, 46, 59, 68, 117, 119
Bullock Committee	2, 22, 25, 26, 30, 83
Burt	2, 11, 20, 31-32, 52, 82, 96, 106-7, 115
Collins	20-21, 25, 27, 28-29, 53-54, 83
Compensatory Education	39, 106, 117
Comprehension	26, 63-65, 110
Co-ordination of Special Provision	19-20, 52-81, 85, 88, 100, 104, 119, 120-1
Counselling	83, 85-87, 111
Craft Lessons	12, 13, 14, 79
Decoding	60, 62, 65
Delinquency	8, 29, 84-86, 93, 95, 116
Dictated Experience Stories	65-66
Discussion	13, 39, 42, 43-44, 47-48, 68-70, 76-77
Disruptive Behaviour	9, 12-14, 31-32, 82, 93-94, 114
DISTAR	22-25
Drama	40, 43-44, 46, 92-93
Dyslexia	53-58, 60
Education Welfare Officers	100, 103-4
Employment	3, 15-18, 23, 38-39, 49, 116
English	67-71
Ethnic Minorities	3, 10, 33, 119
Examinations	14, 37, 49-50, 91-92
Geography	38, 39
Grammar	58
Handicap	17, 35, 79, 85, 113, 115
Headteachers	1, 14, 23-24, 81, 97, 100, 107-8, 109
History	11, 39-41, 115
Home Visits	110-112
Individualized Learning	9, 57, 62
Isle of Wight Survey	23, 32, 34-35, 53, 83-84, 98

Labelling Theory 3, 5-18, 30, 35, 99, 113-116
Language Policy 22, 25-26, 58, 67, 77
Learning Consultant 19, 53-59
Life Skills 37, 38
Low Expectations 3, 7-8, 10, 12, 22, 37, 45, 51, 112
Maladjustment 29, 84, 95, 99
Mathematics 6, 7, 14, 24, 37, 45-46, 71-76, 94
Maturation 6, 21, 28
Medical Officer 96, 101
Morris 17, 22, 25, 80, 105, 115
Named Teachers 59
Neutralization 11, 12, 14, 16
Non-exam Pupils 15, 19, 37-38, 82, 120
Objectives Approach 2, 35-36, 37, 41, 45, 48, 76, 78, 119
Option System 11, 37, 46
Parents 16, 31, 35-36, 49, 105-112, 114-5, 119
Perception 7, 20, 54-55
Peripatetic Remedial Teachers 1, 20-21
Phonics 62-63, 64
Praise 7, 85, 90
Precision Teaching 62, 76, 78
Primary Schools 23-25, 28, 79, 105
Psycholinguistic Guessing Game 56, 62, 65
Psychologists 96-101, 103-4, 121
Readability 25, 29, 61, 67
Reading 5, 20-21, 25, 32, 46-47, 59-67, 105, 116
Recession 1, 17-18, 119-120
Science 29, 42-44, 47, 67, 77-79, 92
Schonell 2, 20
Screening Tests 1-2, 27, 33
Social Studies 38, 39, 40
Social Workers 100, 101-2, 103-4
Special Classes 31-51, 93, 121
Special Educational Needs 4, 18, 23, 35, 84-85, 113, 116-7, 118
Special Schools 3, 29, 36, 48, 98, 100
Specific Learning Difficulties - see Dyxlexia
Spelling 24, 54-58
Stigma 10, 18, 25, 118
Teachers 3, 11, 14, 16, 22-26, 30, 97
Teacher Training 9-10, 26-27, 34, 59-67, 68-79, 89, 92, 120
Tests 2, 8, 19, 27, 28-29, 33, 61-62, 74
Token Economy 88
Transactional Analysis 89-92
Truancy 84-85, 103, 115

U.S.S.R. 108-109
Warnock Report 1, 3, 11, 17, 35, 36, 45, 52-53, 83-84, 101, 108, 113, 115, 117, 120

Withdrawal Groups 19
Work Experience 14-15
Writing 13, 14, 58